AF473893

A LITTLE HISTORY *of the* ROYAL ACADEMY

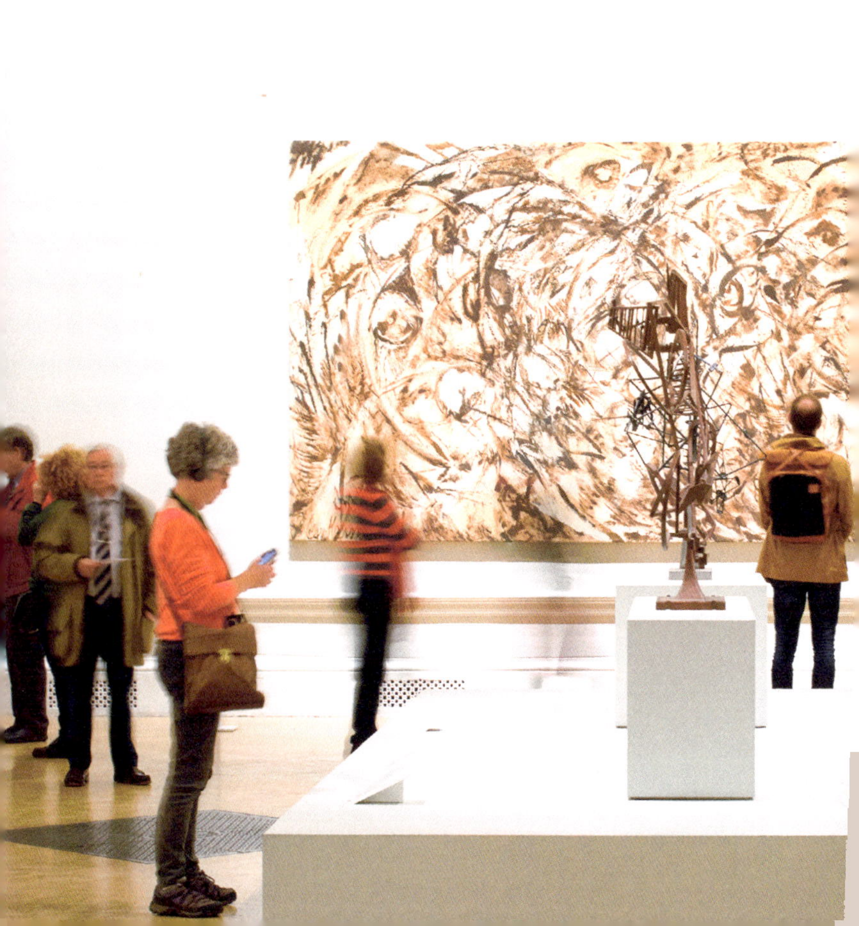

LITTLE HISTORY
of the
ROYAL ACADEMY

PETER SAWBRIDGE

Royal Academy of Arts

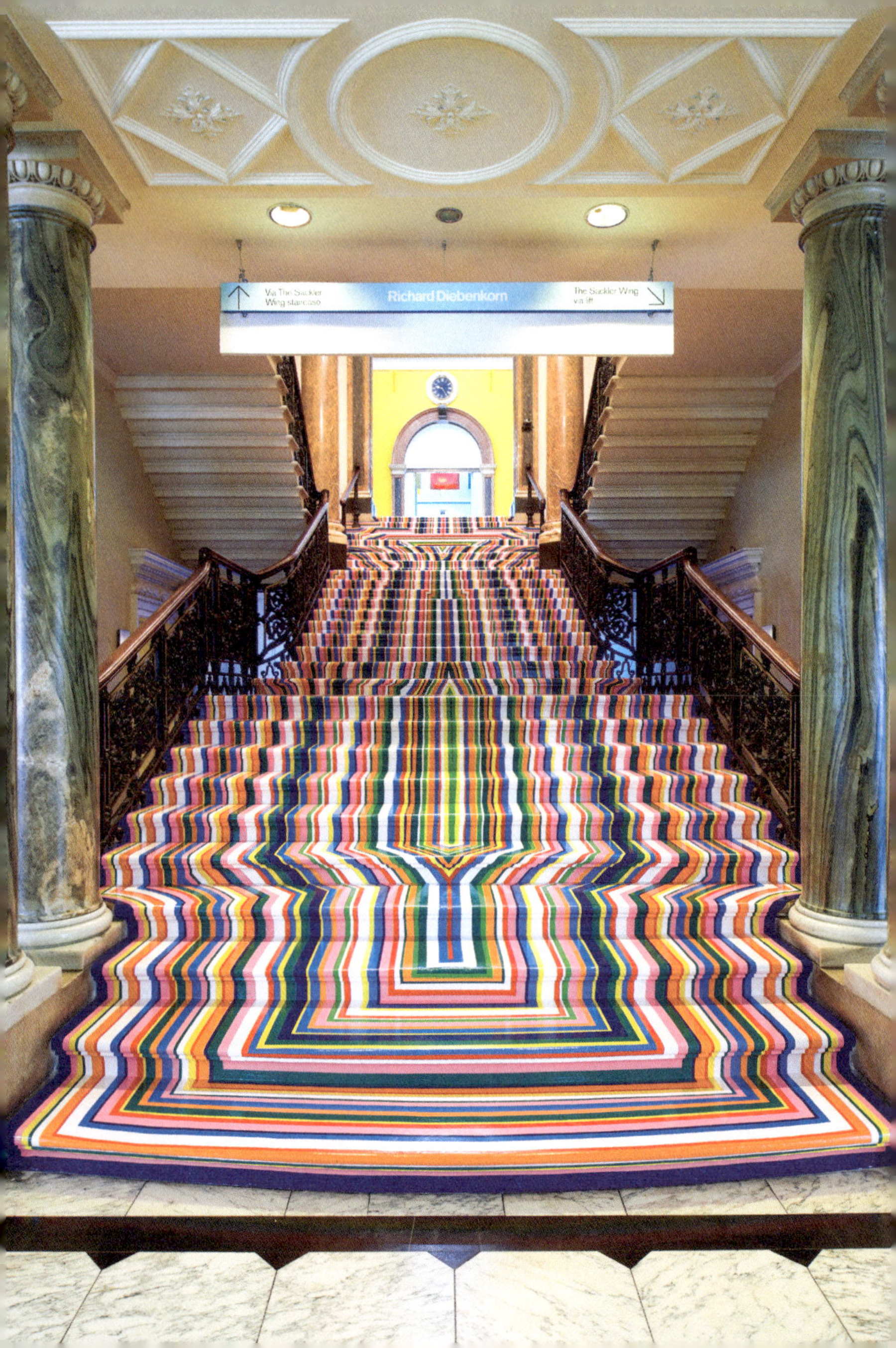
Via The Sackler
Wing staircase
Richard Diebenkorn
The Sackler Wing
via lift

Contents

6 What is the Royal Academy?

16 Pall Mall and Old Somerset House, 1768–79
24 New Somerset House, 1779–1837
40 Trafalgar Square, 1837–67
48 Burlington House, 1868–
66 The Earlier Twentieth Century
76 The Modern Academy, 1976–

93 Further Reading
96 List of Illustrations
100 Index

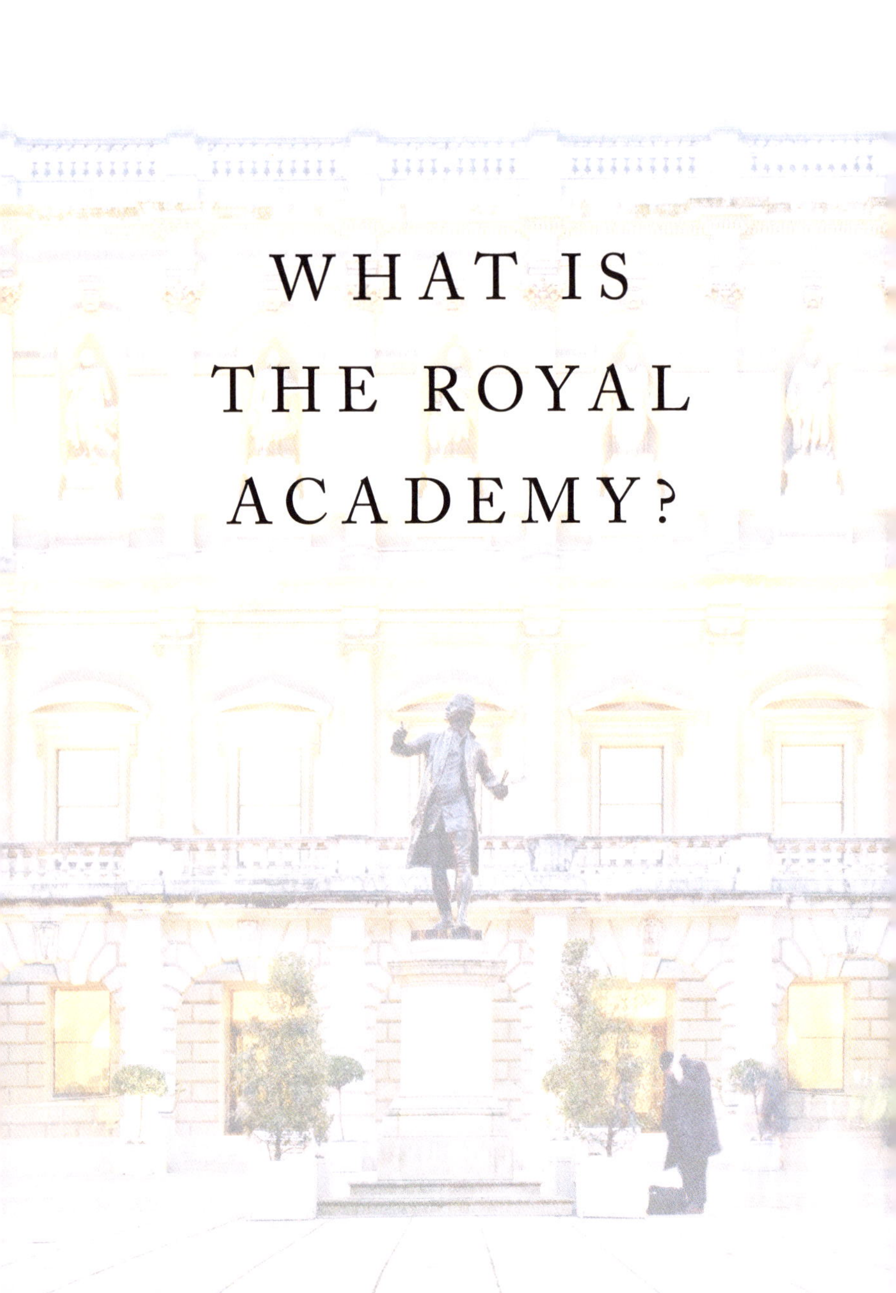

WHAT IS THE ROYAL ACADEMY?

The Royal Academy is many things to many people. To most, it is a place to join friends to see some of London's most highly regarded art exhibitions, to have something to eat or a drink, and to buy the show's catalogue and something unusual and imaginative from the shop. In fact, it is a great deal more than this, and indeed, the international loan exhibitions that have brought it acclaim are a relatively recent addition to its activities.

Perhaps we might define it at the outset by saying that it is a royal institution of eighteenth-century constitution, still run by and for its self-selecting member artists, the Royal Academicians, who alone are entitled to place the prestigious letters 'RA' after their names. Elected into distinct categories – painters, architects, sculptors, engravers, draughtsmen and printmakers – these Royal Academicians can only ever number around eighty. 'Of fair moral characters, of high reputation in their several professions; at least five-and-twenty years of age; resident in Great Britain, and not members of any other society of artists established in London', to quote the Instrument of Foundation signed by King George III, the Royal Academicians are entitled to hang six of their own works for sale in each year's Summer Exhibition; a committee of them selects other works from a huge public submission to hang alongside these.

On election, Royal Academicians are expected to present to the Academy's collection an example of their output, a Diploma Work, and to sit on its various

The Library of the Royal Academy, Burlington House

Overleaf: an iPad drawing course in the Life Room as part of the Academic Programme, 2017

committees until they reach their seventy-fifth birthdays, at which point they become Senior Royal Academicians. The Academicians select from within their membership the Academy's Officers – a President (PRA), a Treasurer and a Keeper – and a Council, 'which shall have the entire direction and management of all the business of the Society'. A number of artists who live outside the British Isles are elected as Honorary Royal Academicians, and Honorary Fellows can be elected, too, from other fields of activity.

The Royal Academy Schools are led by the Keeper and offer a free education to art students, with running costs funded by the proceeds of the Summer Exhibition. Around twenty students a year join the Schools from many hundreds of applicants to follow a three-year postgraduate course. The staff and Professors of the Royal Academy Schools work with the students alongside numerous visiting artists, some of them Royal Academicians. The historic Life Room in the Royal Academy Schools is still in regular use, and indeed the furniture historian Simon Jervis has recently suggested that some elements of its furnishings may be older than the Academy itself. It is rather wonderful when in that room to think that you might be sitting on a seat once occupied by Blake, Constable or Turner.

Headed by the Secretary and Chief Executive, who is nowadays not a Royal Academician, the Academy's professional staff delivers a programme of international loan exhibitions and accompanying

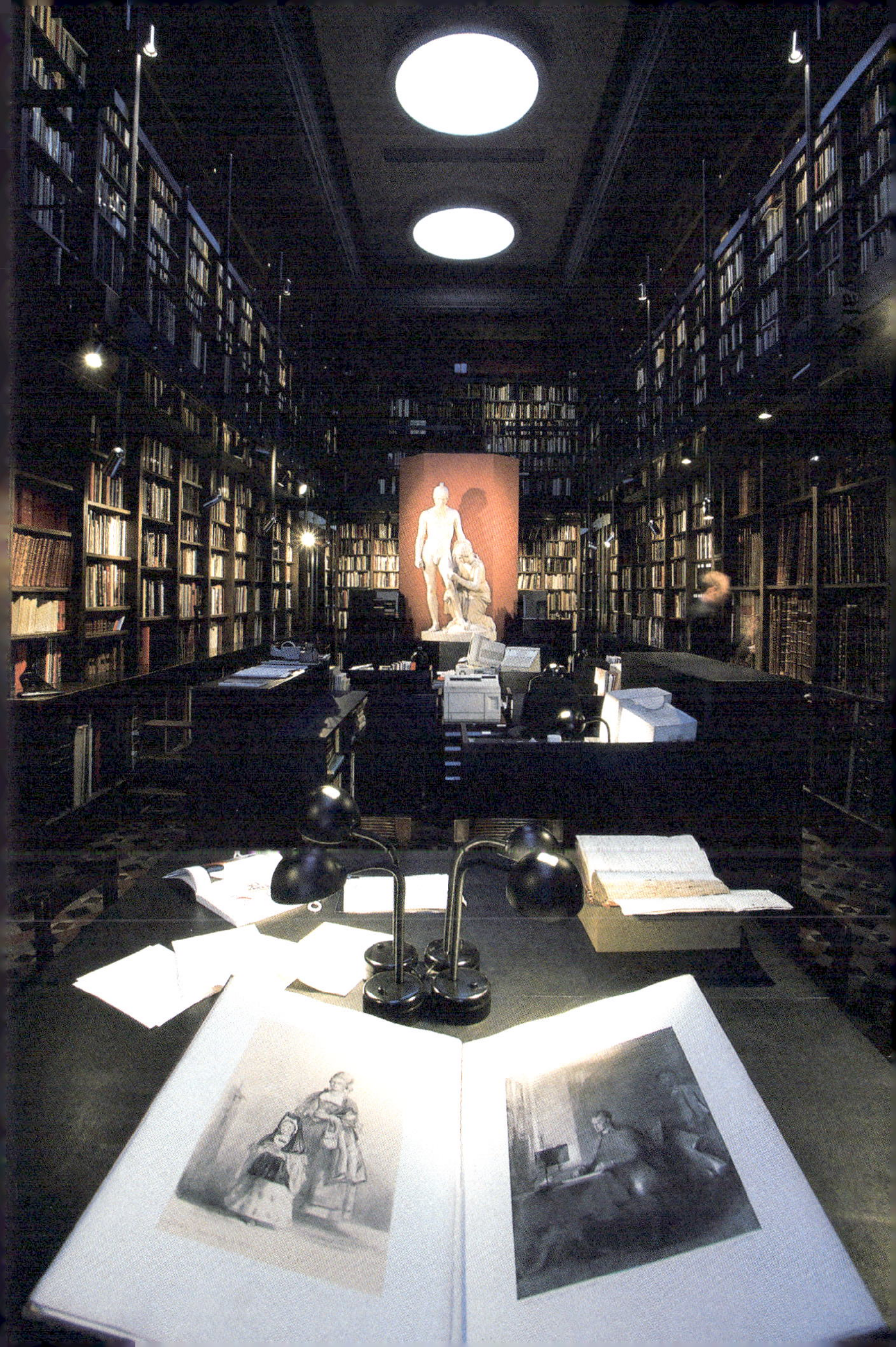

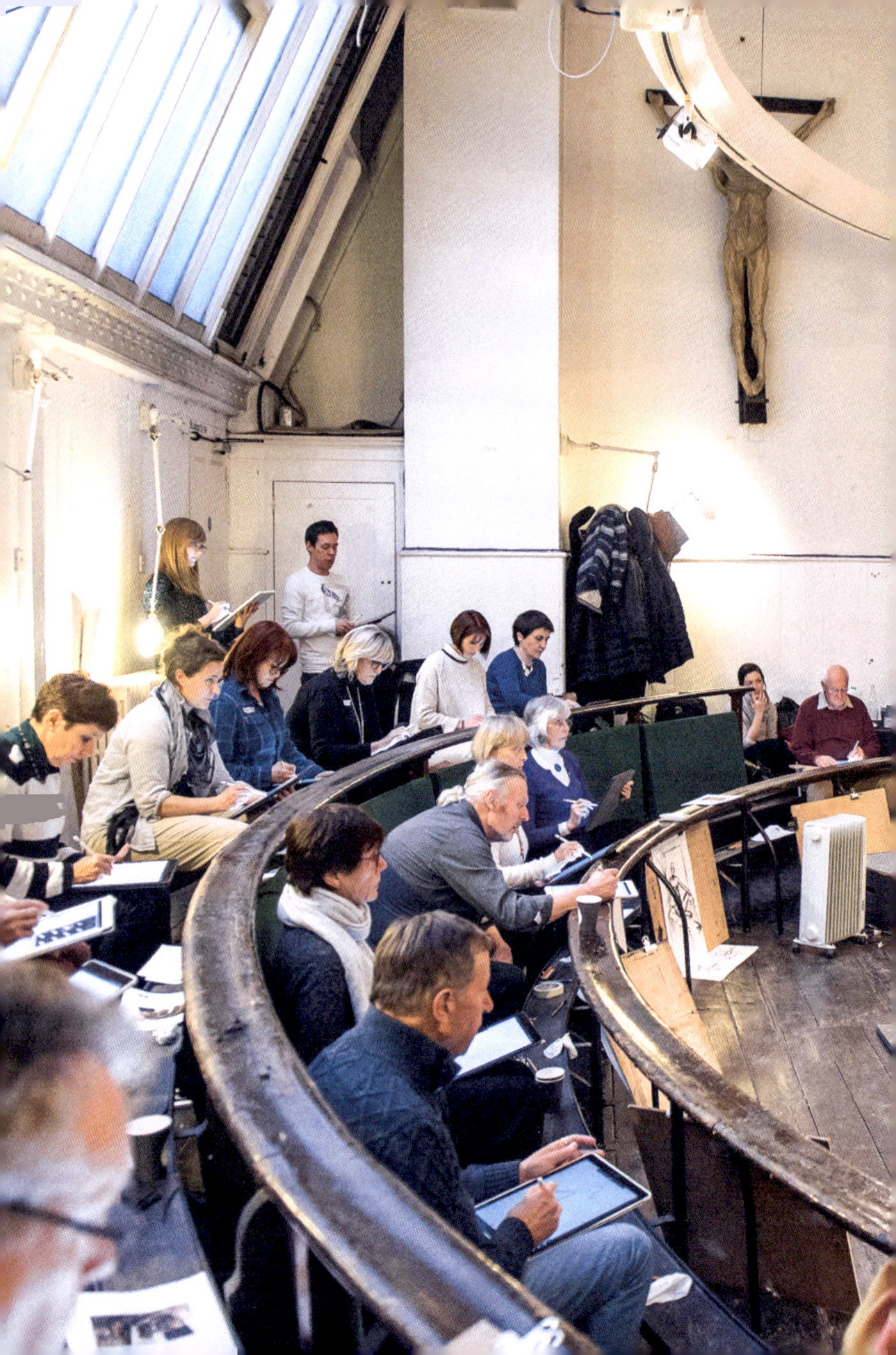

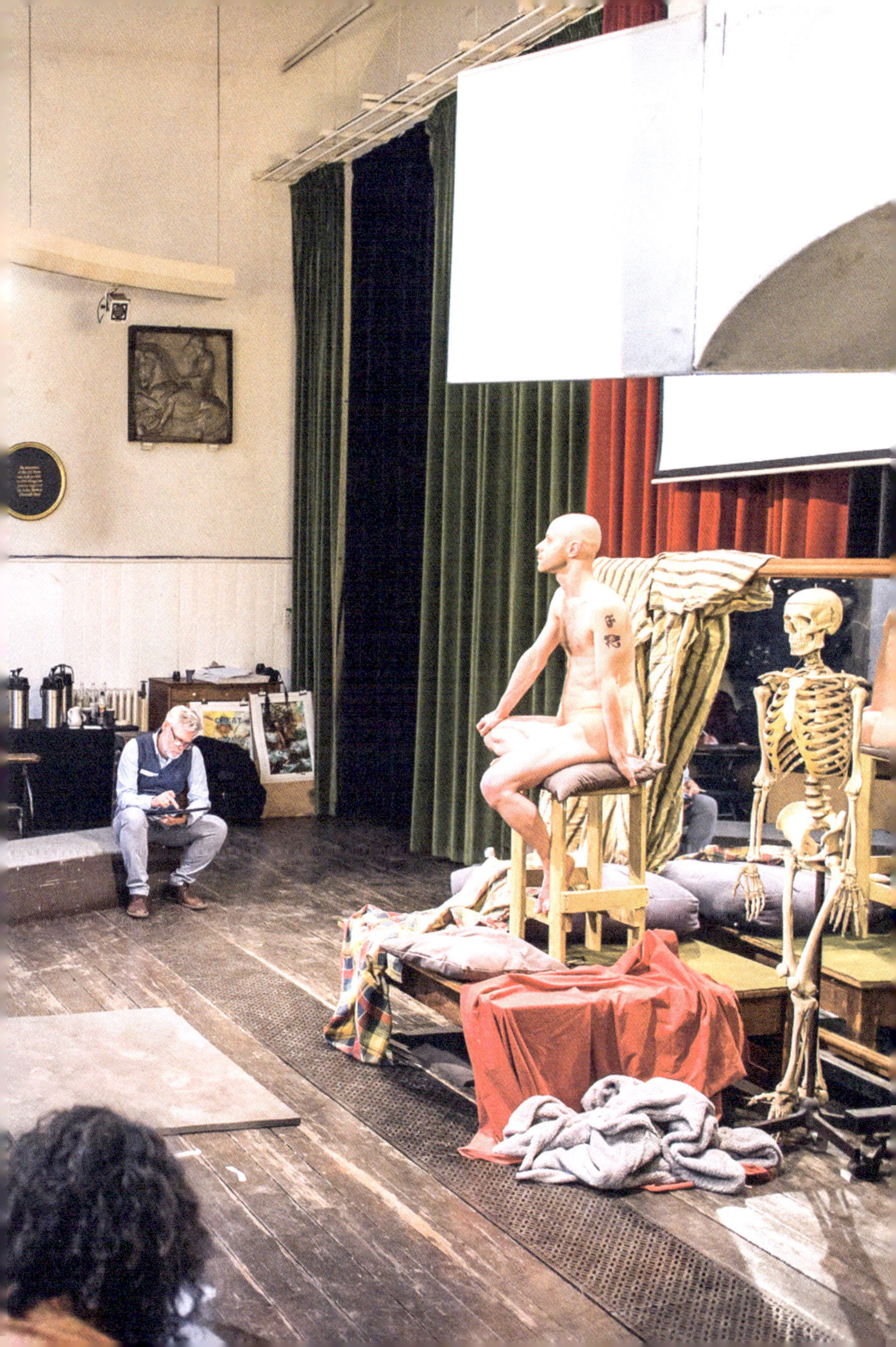

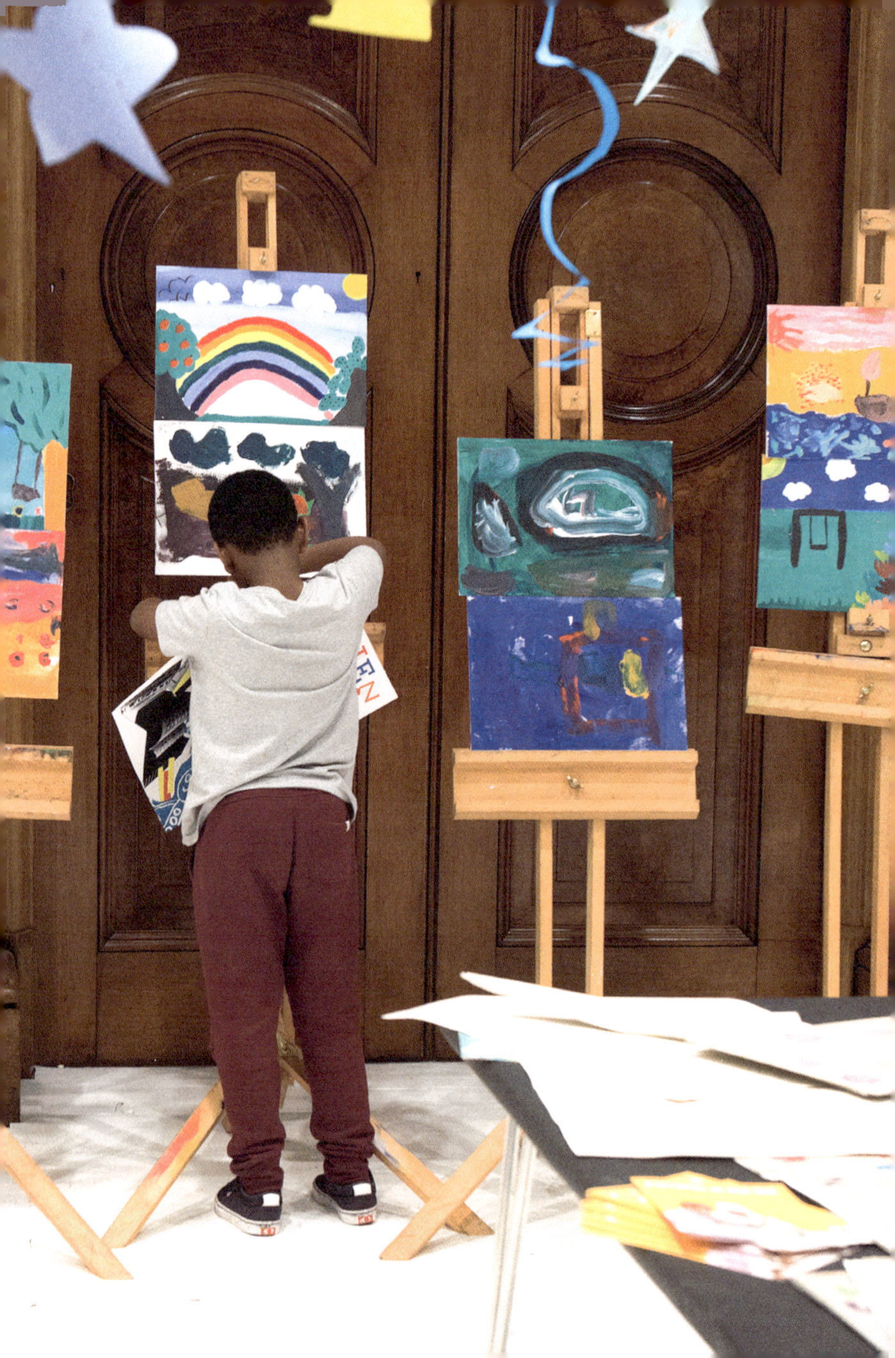

A children's learning workshop

Overleaf: General Assembly of the Royal Academicians, 19 March 2018. Photograph by Johnnie Shand Kydd (a key appears on pages 94–95)

publications, debates, lectures, courses and classes, and cares for a rich collection of paintings, sculpture, drawings and prints, and a remarkable library.

All these strands of activity – many going on behind the scenes at Burlington House – come together to create a complex organisation that carries out its eighteenth-century mission, 'promoting the Arts of Design', to this day. This small volume is intended to chart the key points of the Academy's 250-year story, touching on how its homes and some of its characters have made it what it is, and to encourage those wanting to learn more to turn to the list of comprehensive studies that appears on page 93.

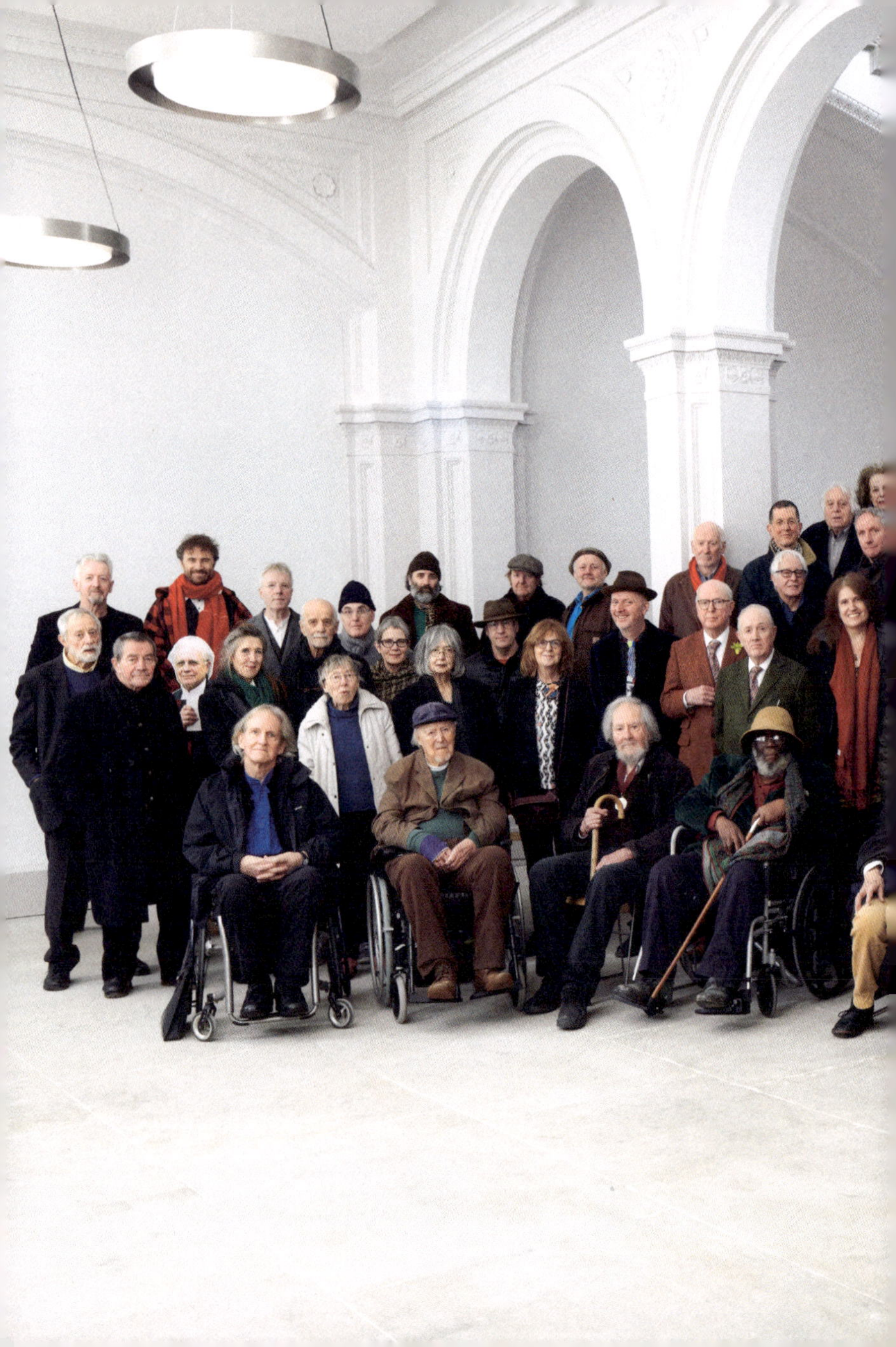

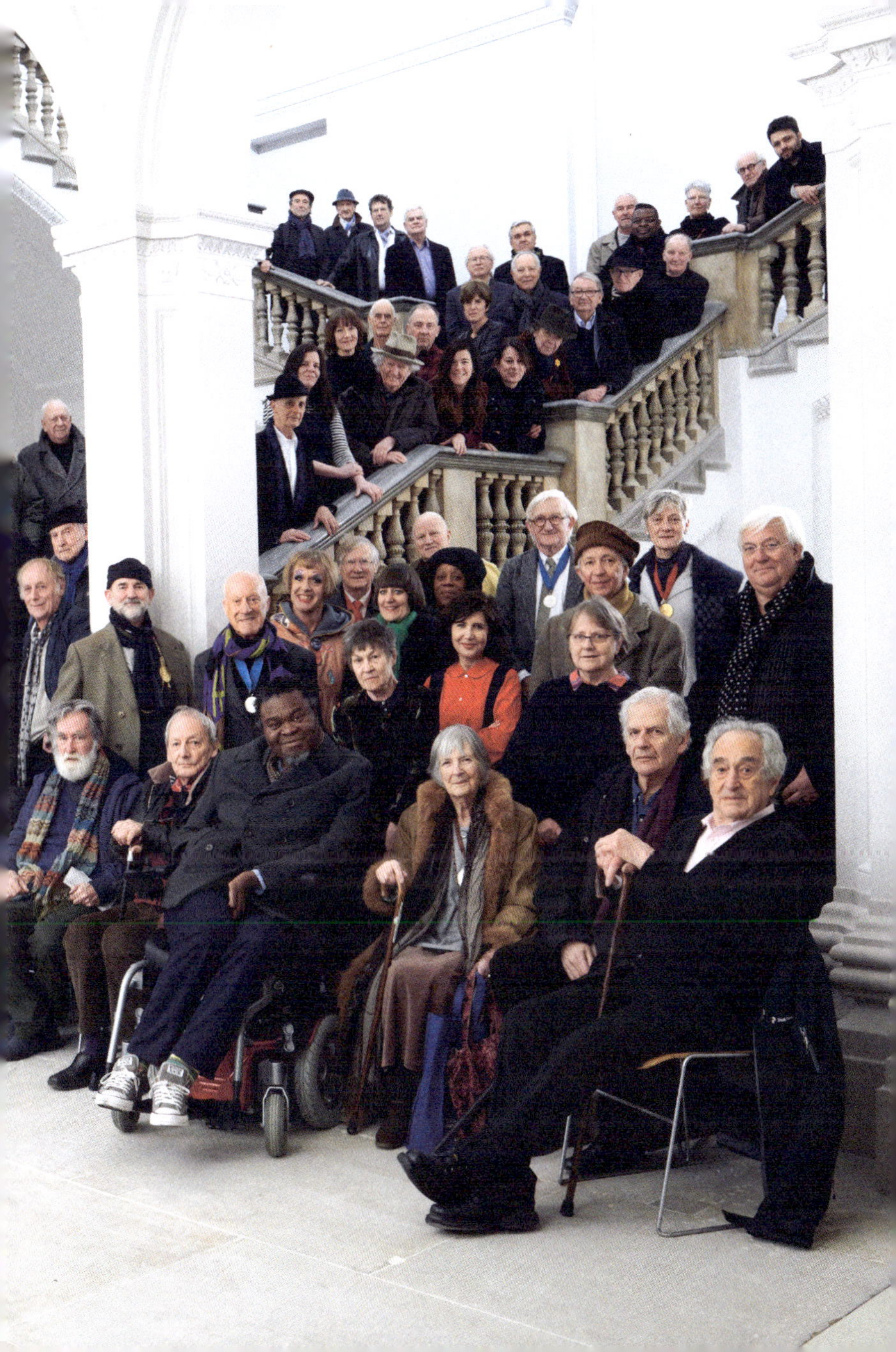

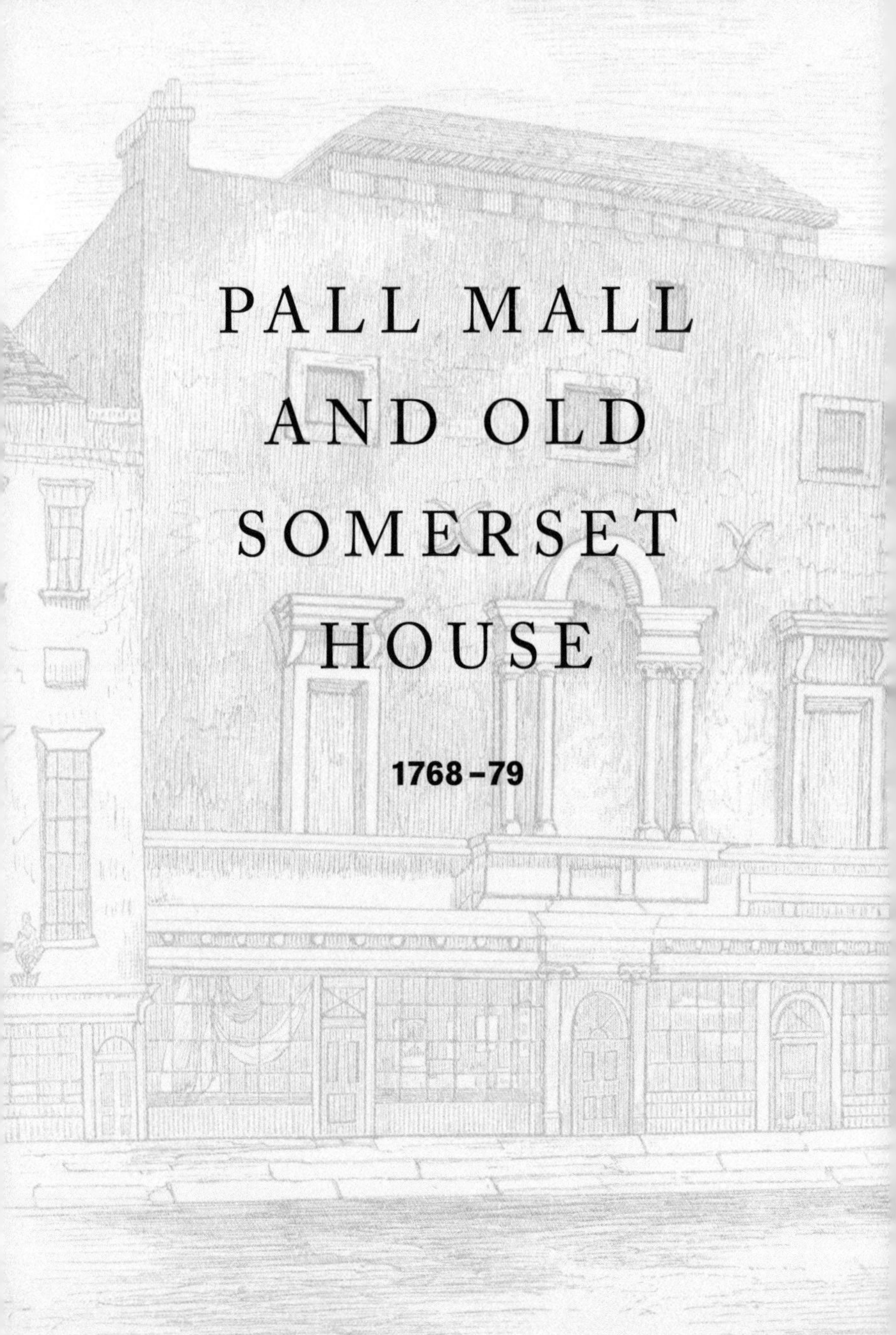

PALL MALL AND OLD SOMERSET HOUSE

1768–79

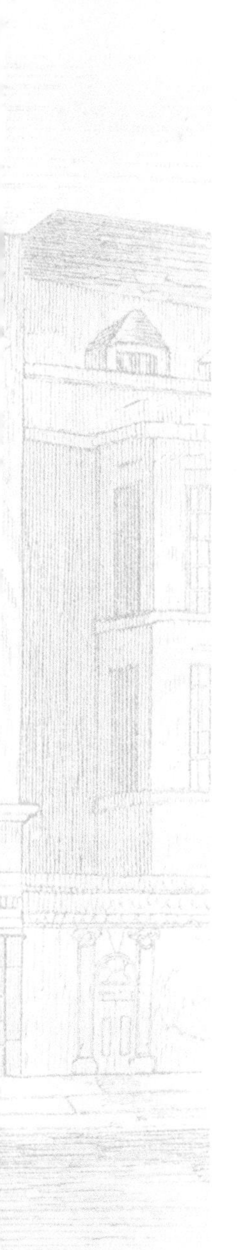

London's Royal Academy is a comparative newcomer as academies go. The first academy was founded by Plato in Athens in the fourth century BC, although his was probably more of a debating forum than a school for artists. Cosimo and Lorenzo de' Medici followed the classical Greek philosopher's example in Renaissance Florence, as did the painters of Rome, with their Compagnia di San Luca, later the Accademia di San Luca, and King Louis XIV of France, with his Parisian Académie Royale de Peinture et de Sculpture. From at least the mid-seventeenth century, British artists hankered after such an institution to give them the professional standing they craved. Although a number of loose associations were formed, generally in the capital, it wasn't until 1768 that the Royal Academy was established by King George III.

A small group of artists led by George III's architectural tutor, Sir William Chambers, visited St James's Palace that November to explain to the King their plan for a new institution to be backed financially by the sovereign that intended to use the revenue generated by an annual exhibition, 'open to all Artists of distinguished merit', to pay for the activities of an art school. The following week, on 10 December 1768, the King signed the Instrument of Foundation: 'I approve of this Plan, let it be put into execution.' An exact contemporary of Chambers, but a painter, Sir Joshua Reynolds was persuaded to stand as the new institution's first President, with Chambers appointed its first Treasurer personally by the King.

The Royal Academy first opened its doors at 125 Pall Mall, a modest building that had formerly housed an auctioneer's business near what is today Trafalgar Square. The Annual Exhibitions, meetings and dinners were held there, although from 1771 the Royal Academy Schools and various offices also

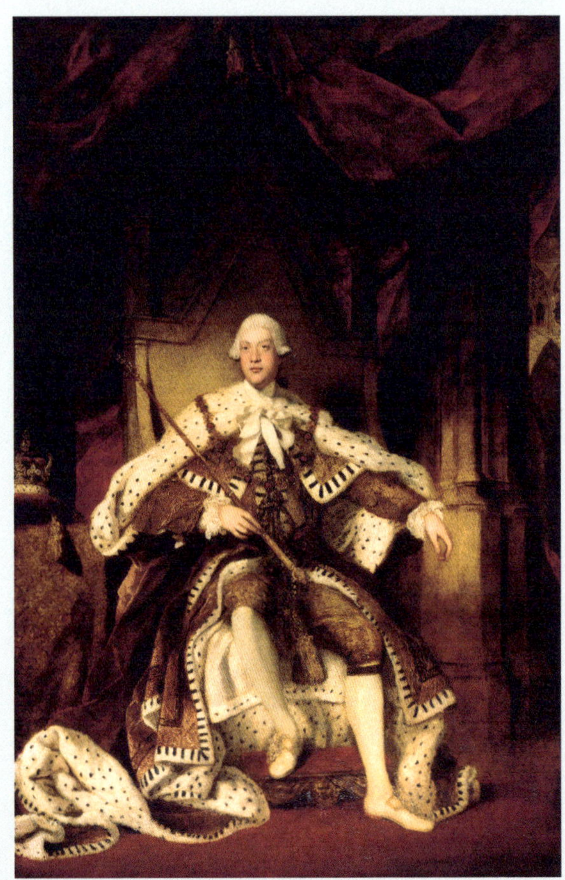

Sir Joshua Reynolds PRA, *King George III*, 1779

Sir Joshua Reynolds PRA, *Sir William Chambers*, c. 1780

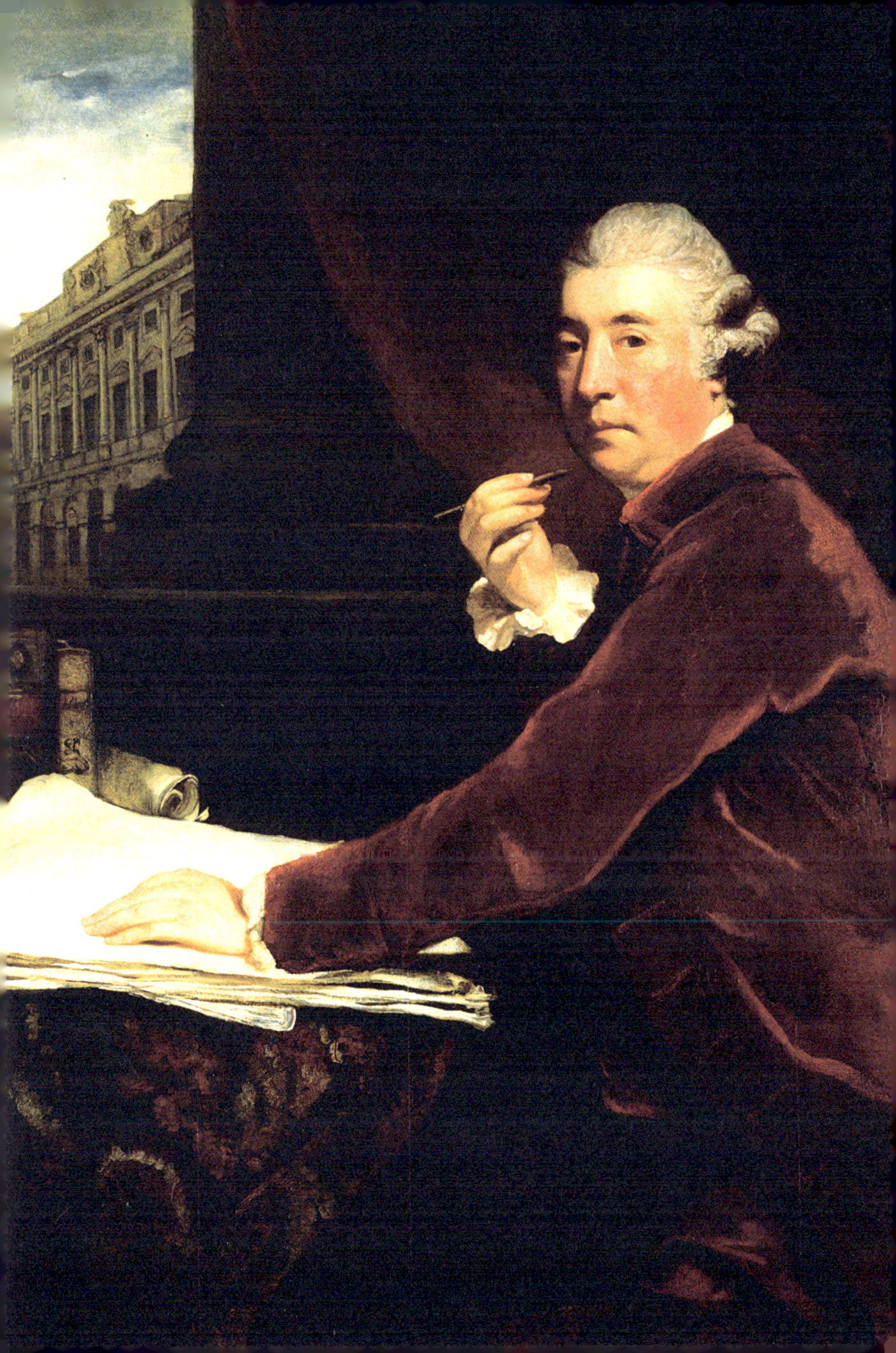

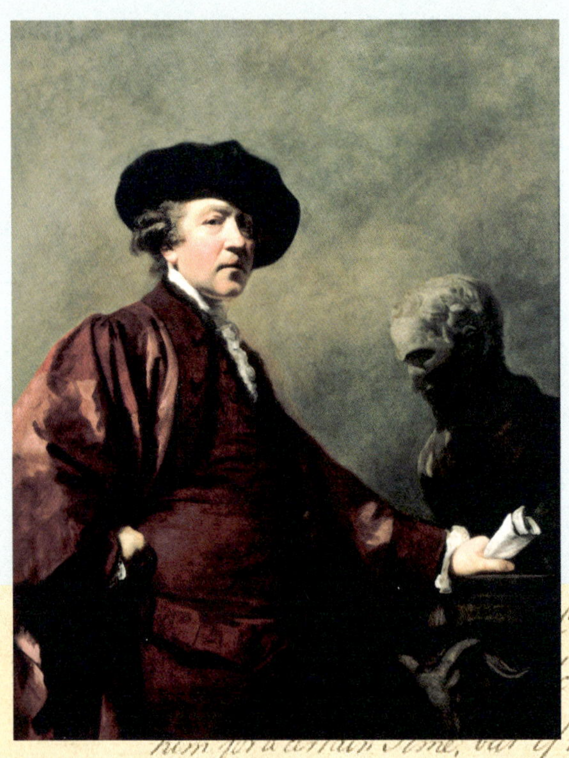

Sir Joshua Reynolds PRA, *Self-portrait*, *c.* 1780

The Instrument of Foundation (detail)

Overleaf: Johann Zoffany RA, *The Academicians of the Royal Academy*, 1771–72

Council upon Comp

cademy, to Expel

he be once Expel

readmitted in to the Royal Schools

27°

All Modes of Elections shall be regulated by

Society hereafter to be made for that Purp

I approve of this Plan, let it

St James's
Dec.r 10th 1768.

George

made use of a set of faded royal apartments that had been designed by Inigo Jones at Old Somerset House. Reynolds gave the first of his *Discourses*, his influential lectures on art to the students of the Royal Academy, at Pall Mall on 2 January 1769.

In a group portrait of the Royal Academicians made in 1771–72 by Johann Zoffany, who was nominated a Foundation Member by George III in 1768, Sir Joshua stands prominently in the centre of the group holding his ear-trumpet (you will have seen Alfred Drury's bronze statue of him on your way into Burlington House). The items Zoffany includes make the room closely resemble the Academy's present-day Life Room, although it is thought to have been at Old Somerset House. Zoffany sits on the far left, palette in hand. The American artist Benjamin West, who was to serve as PRA from 1792, leans back elegantly immediately behind Zoffany. Chambers stands next to Reynolds, listening to Francis Milner Newton, the Academy's first Secretary, and the model is set by George Michael Moser, the first Keeper, with advice from various onlookers. Two female Royal Academicians were prevented from attending life classes for reasons of decorum, so Zoffany included them in unfinished portraits hanging on the wall, Mary Moser, the Keeper's daughter, on the right and Angelica Kauffman on the left.

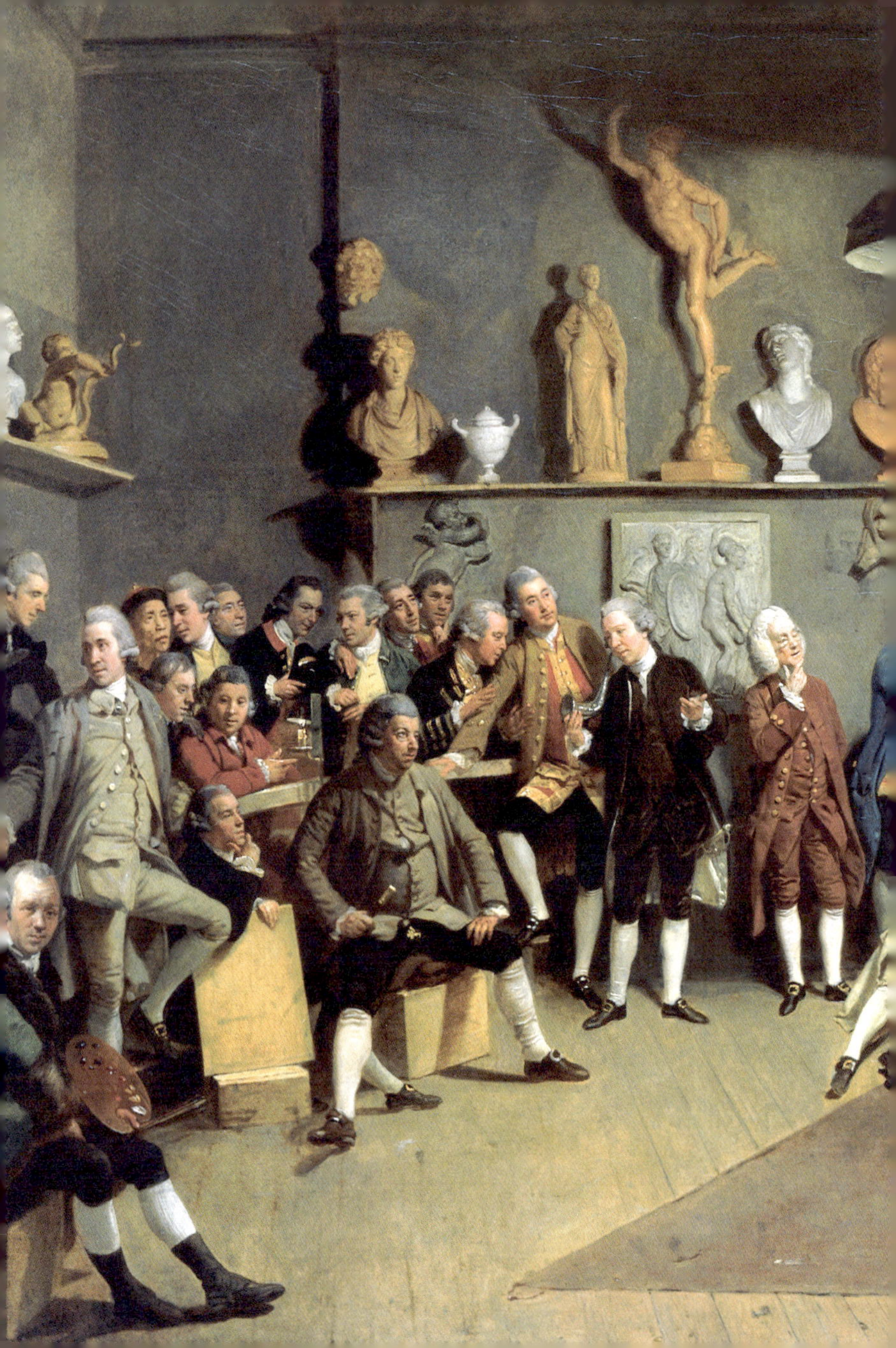

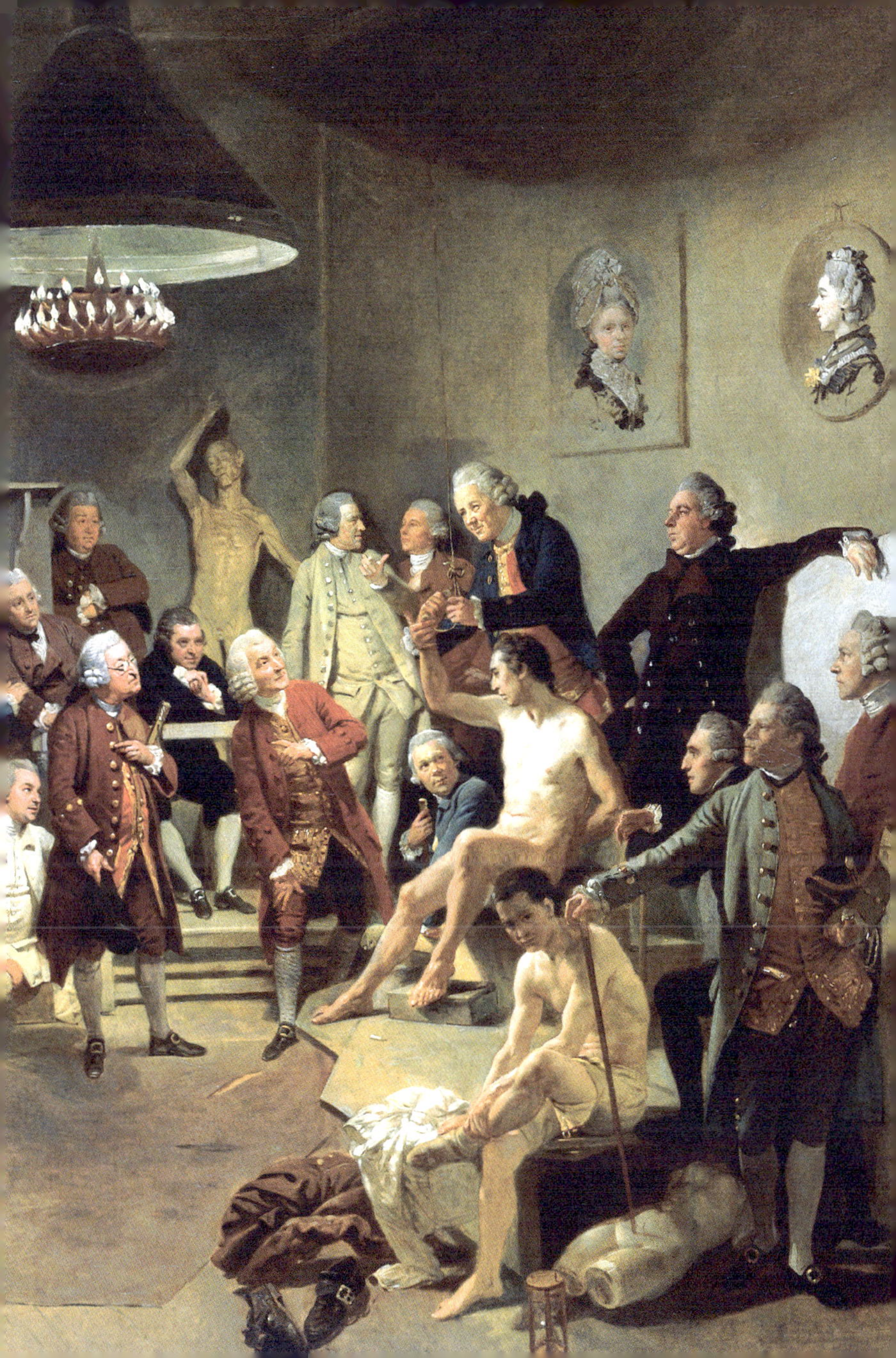

NEW SOMERSET HOUSE

1779–1837

The Annual Exhibition at Pall Mall grew quickly in scale and popularity, and received healthy interest and attendances from the start. In 1779, a decade under its belt, the Royal Academy moved into the imposing Strand buildings of Chambers's New Somerset House, to the handsome exhibition rooms occupied today by the Courtauld Institute Galleries. Chambers had been commissioned to build a set of new government buildings on the Thames-side site of Old Somerset House, and he fulfilled his brief with a magnificent classical palace. In 1795 Henry Singleton painted the Academicians assembled there, West in the President's throne, with Mary Moser and Angelica Kauffman permitted to be present this time, behind him, the gathering dominated by a plaster cast of the Vatican's antique sculpture of Laocoön and his ill-fated sons.

In *c.* 1800 Thomas Rowlandson, a former student of the Royal Academy Schools, caricatured men who tried to look up women's skirts as they climbed Chambers's dizzying oval 'stare case' to see the Annual Exhibition in the top-lit Great Room. All the works on show, from substantial landscapes to the full-length royal portraits that dominated the crammed hangs, leaving barely an inch between their frames, had made their perilous ascent to this top storey too. The Great Room, whose doorway bore the inscription 'Let no Stranger to the Muses enter' in ancient Greek, was of a scale that permitted many more works to be hung than in Pall Mall, which in turn increased the number of visitors considerably.

Henry Singleton, *The Royal Academicians in General Assembly*, 1795

Thomas Rowlandson, *The Exhibition 'Stare-Case', Somerset House*, c. 1800

This was all good news for the fledgling institution, and thus for the monarch, who had undertaken to support it financially. Before long, sales of tickets and, from 1798, catalogues to the Annual Exhibition were bringing in sufficient revenue to keep the ship afloat. Painters and sculptors were initially encouraged to conform to the strict hierarchy of genres that Sir Joshua had exhorted them to adopt in his *Discourses*: history painting at the zenith, followed by portraiture, genre painting, landscape and still-life, in that order. But as the new century approached, the old divisions began to break down and the genres began gradually to melt into one another.

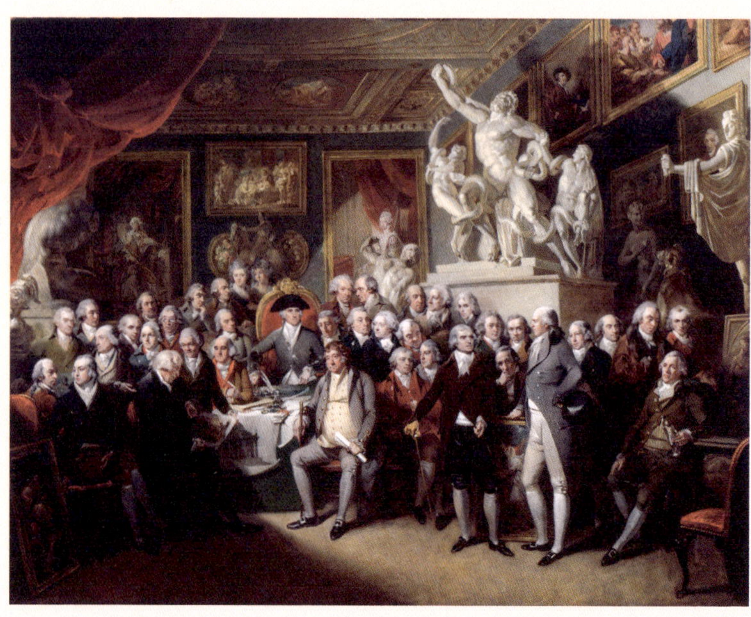

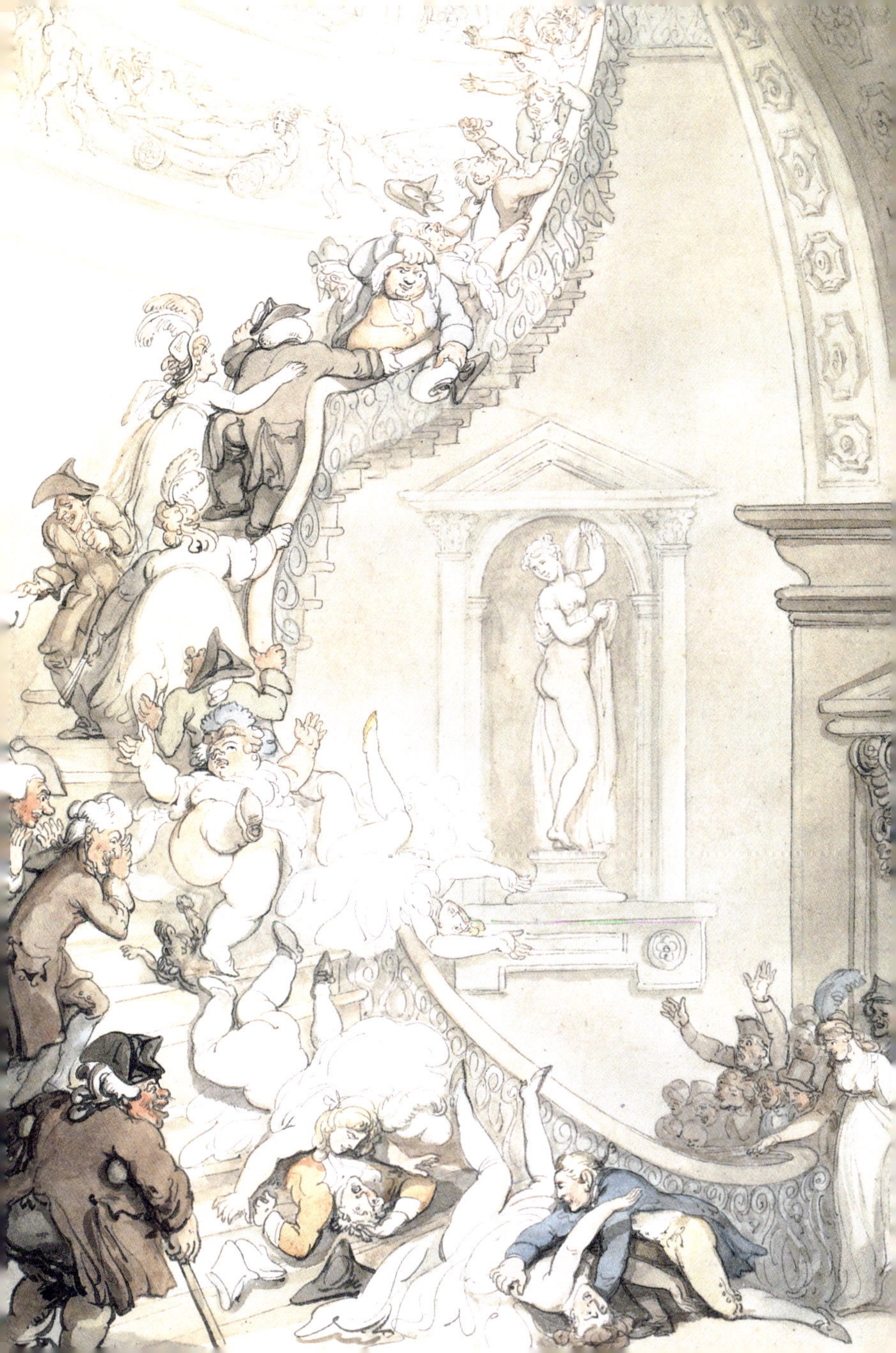

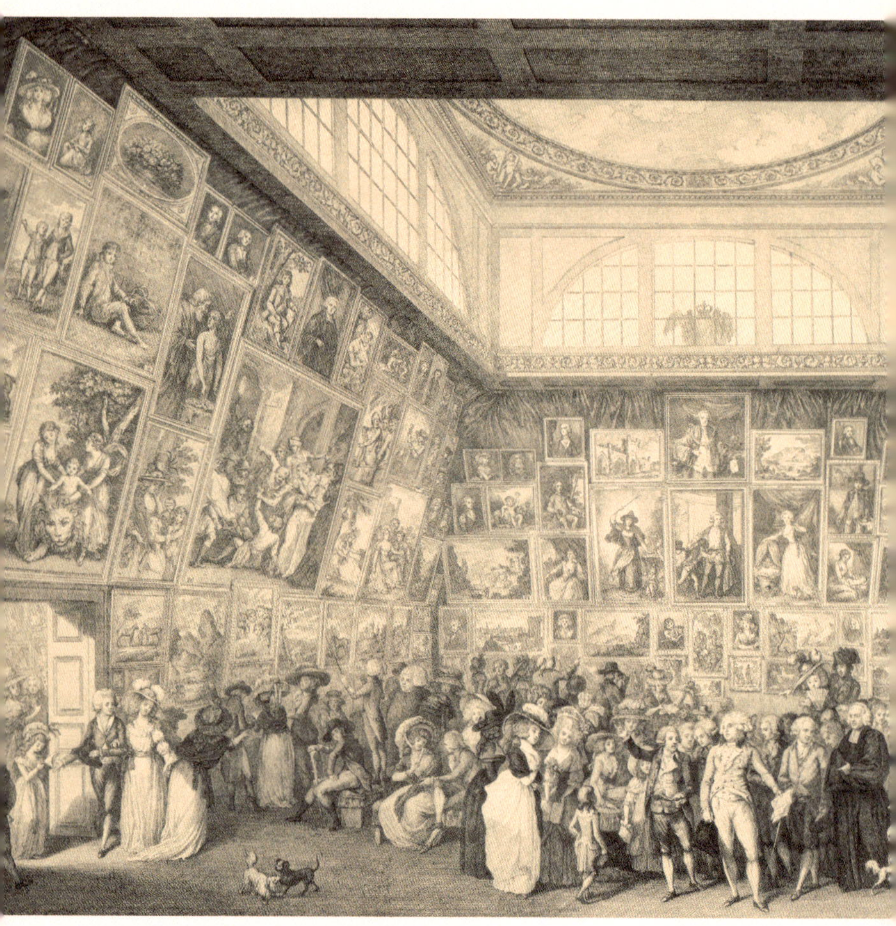

Pietro Antonio Martini, after Johann Heinrich Ramberg, *The Exhibition of the Royal Academy*, 1787

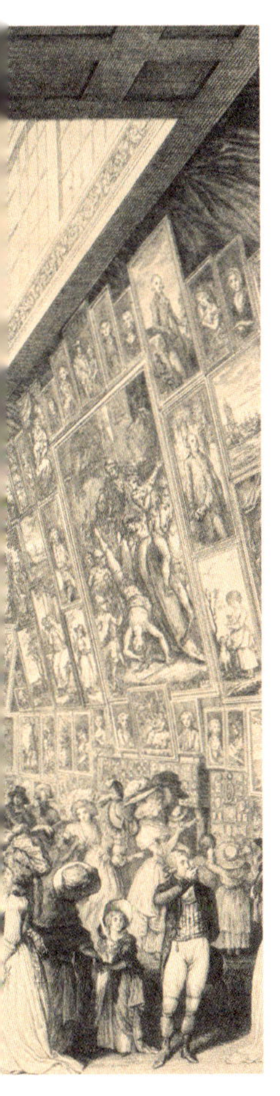

In the waning decades of the eighteenth century, the portraitist Thomas Gainsborough, never a contented Royal Academician, painted landscapes that heralded the coming romantic era and its fascination with the wildness of nature. He famously squabbled with the hanging committees of several Annual Exhibitions in the early 1780s about their placement of his works, and then abandoned the Academy altogether, thereafter showing his work at his own house in Pall Mall.

This loosening of the hierarchy of genres culminated in the intermingling of history painting and landscape achieved by J. M. W. Turner, who was elected an Associate Royal Academician (ARA) at the age of only 24. *Dolbadern Castle*, his Diploma Work, evokes the awe-inspiring immensity of the castle's natural surroundings, which render the human figures in the foreground negligible in both scale and importance.

John Constable, Turner's great rival as a landscape artist, had a different approach, one that was to prevent his election as an Associate Royal Academician until he was in his forties. In his depictions of rural life in the Vale of Dedham, such as his Diploma Work, *A Boat Passing a Lock*, and *The Leaping Horse*, he skilfully orchestrates weather, light and the Suffolk landscape of his boyhood, bringing to his everyday subjects a uniquely fresh naturalism and a perhaps unexpected spiritual depth.

Turner's performances at Varnishing Days for the Annual Exhibition are well known, and have been

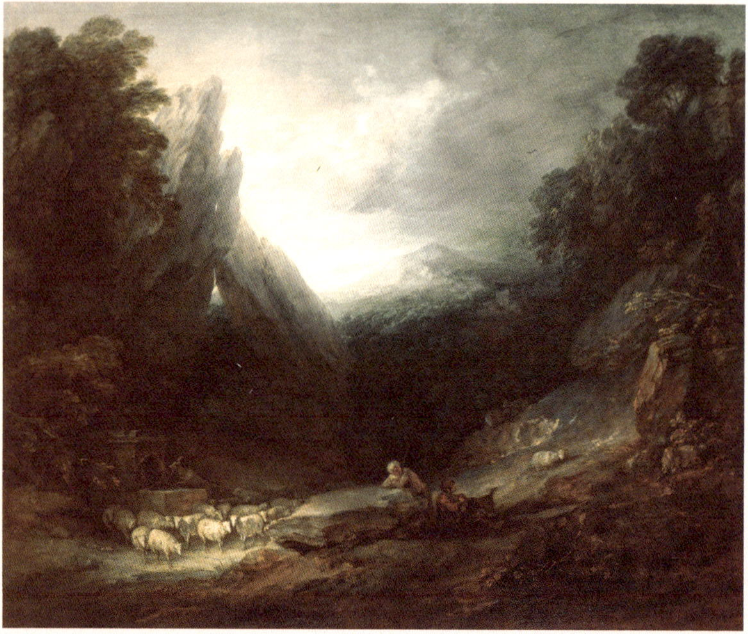

Thomas Gainsborough RA, *Romantic Landscape with Sheep at a Spring*, c. 1783

J. M. W. Turner RA, *Dolbadern Castle*, 1800

John Constable RA, *A Boat Passing a Lock*, 1826

Overleaf: John Constable RA, *The Leaping Horse*, 1825

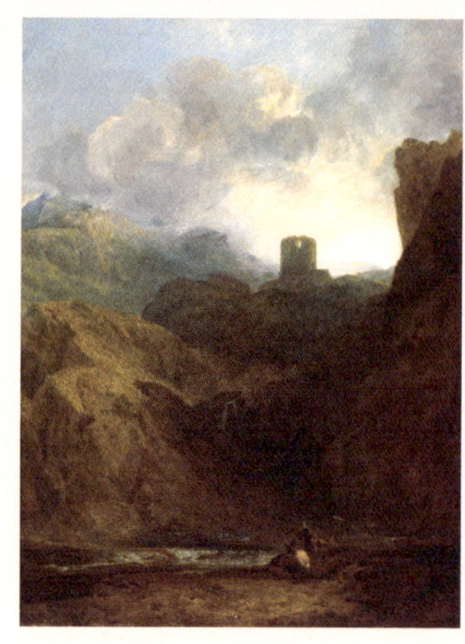

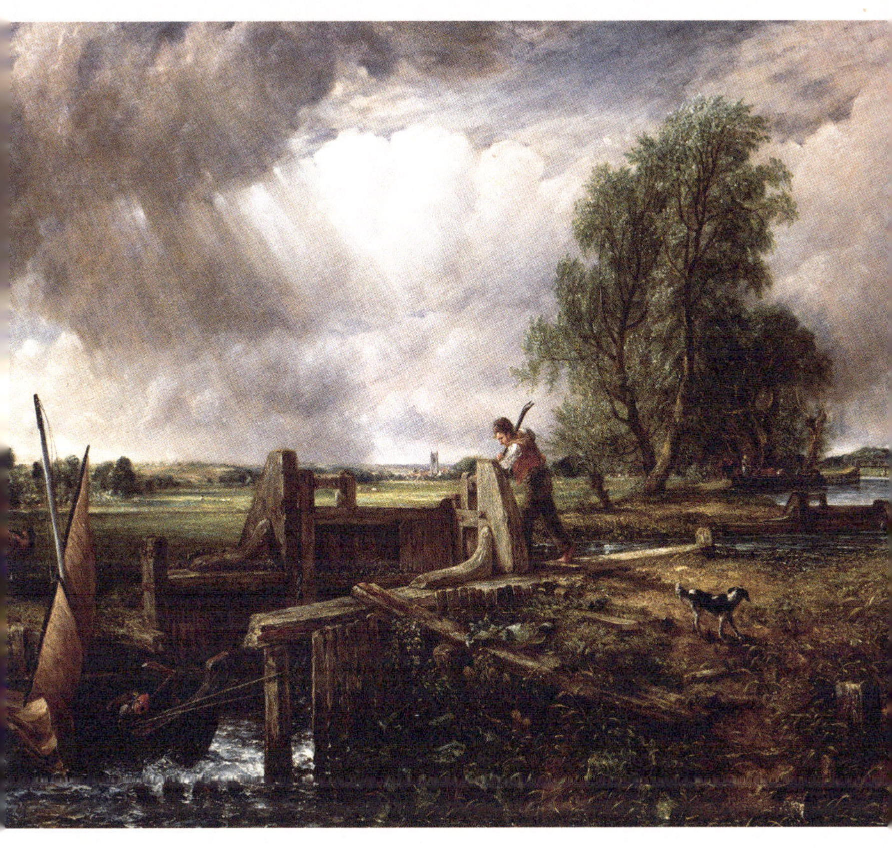

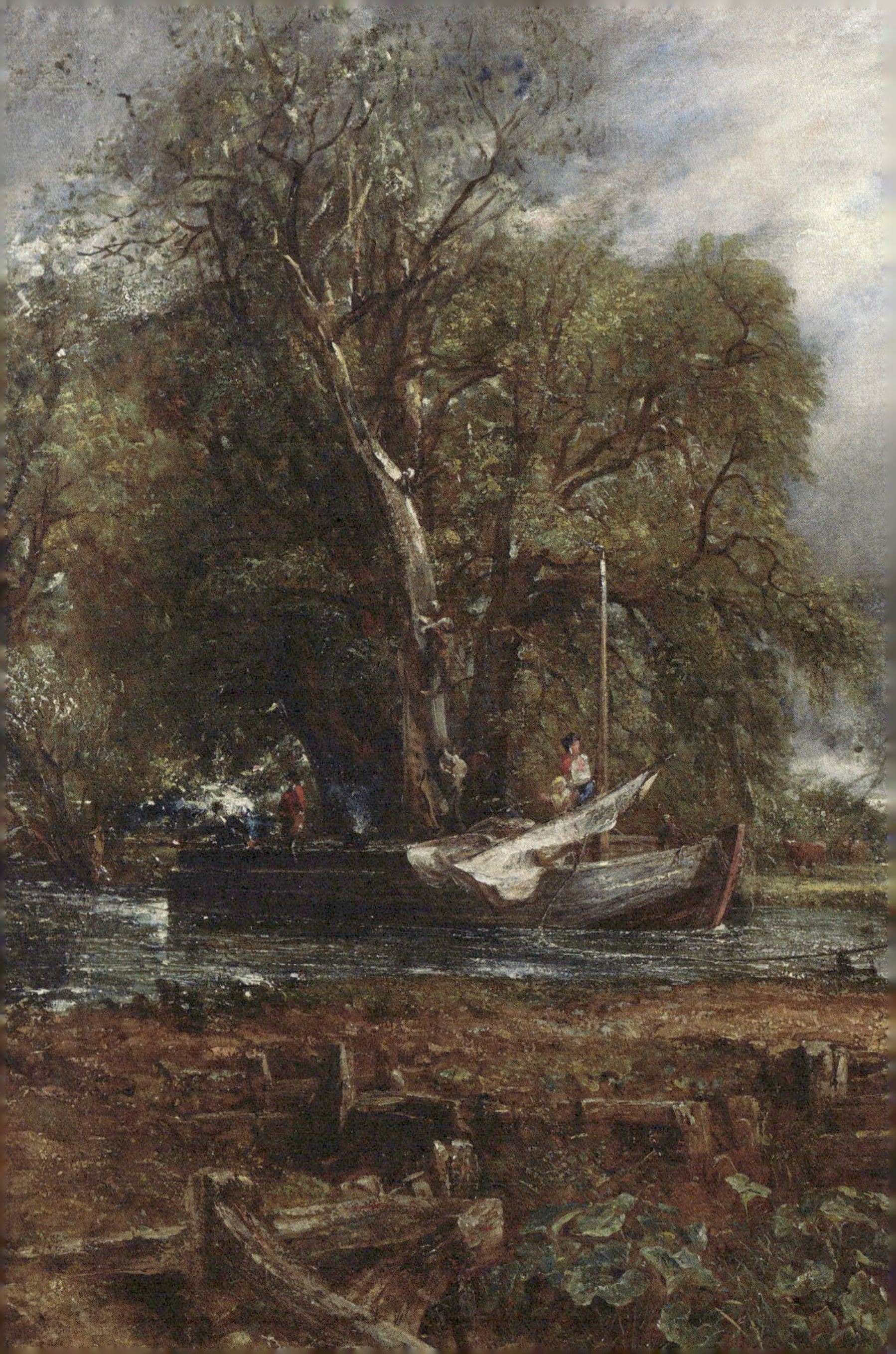

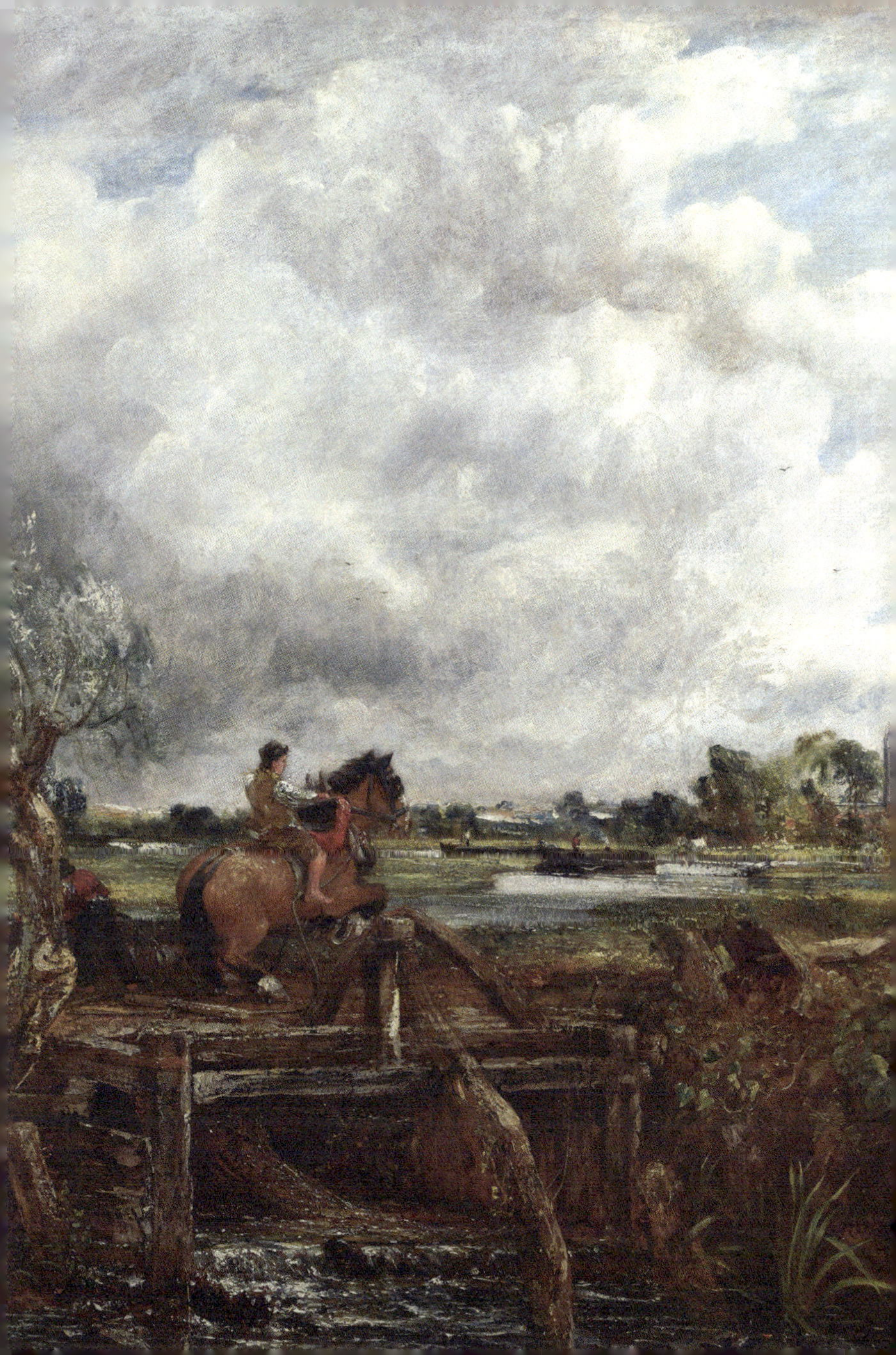

made more so by Mike Leigh's 2014 film *Mr Turner*. Varnishing Days – opportunities for Royal Academicians to make adjustments to their works when all the selected pictures were hanging – were the Royal Academicians' first chance to see where in the galleries their paintings had been placed by the committee. As Gainsborough's wranglings with hanging committees reveal, this could greatly affect an artist's prestige. Too high, or 'skyed', and no detail could be seen. Insufficiently prominent among a wall of other works, or next to a doorway, and a picture

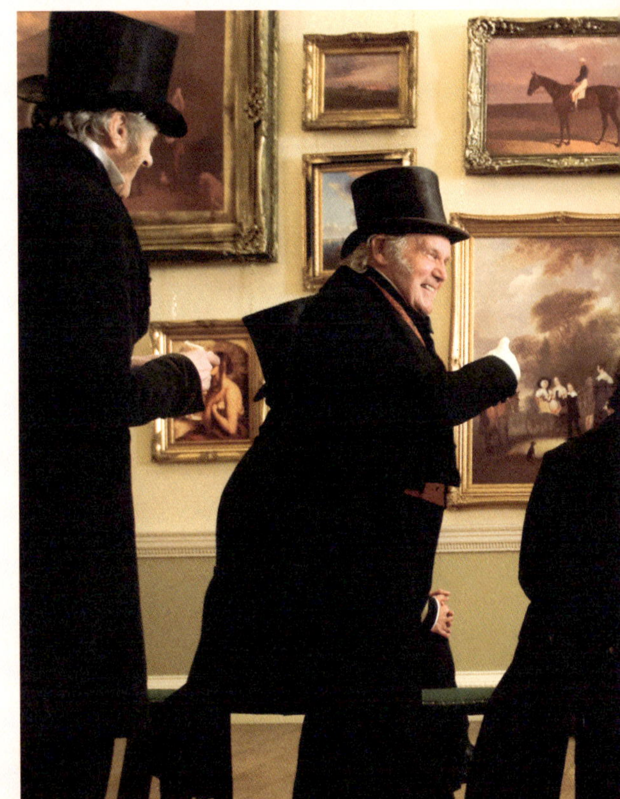

A still from Mike Leigh's 2014 film *Mr Turner*, showing Timothy Spall in the title role, retouching a work on one of the Varnishing Days at the Annual Exhibition

might be overlooked. On these occasions Turner dazzled his fellow Royal Academicians with virtuoso touches of paint, reputedly making his works spring to life and dominate those adjacent in a kind of pictorial sorcery.

West resigned as President in 1805, but was returned to office the following year, his successor, the architect James Wyatt, having failed to balance the expectations of his many architectural clients around the country with the Academy's lengthy meetings. West suffered at Court, having perhaps

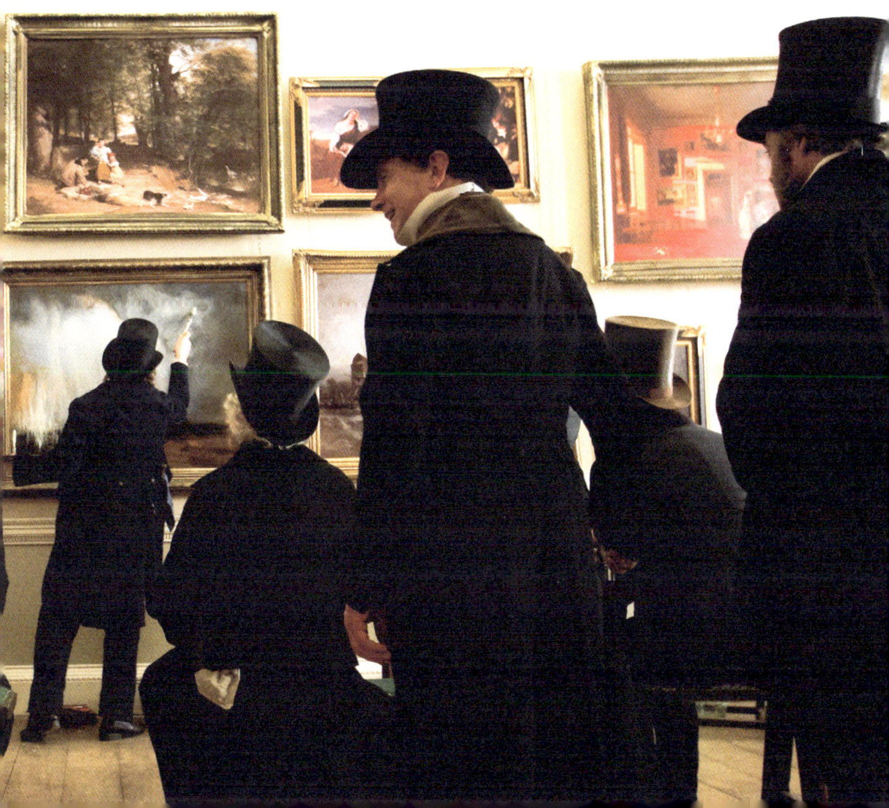

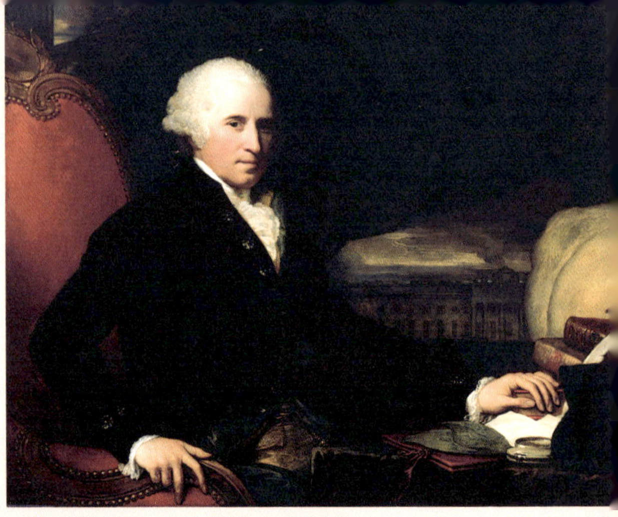

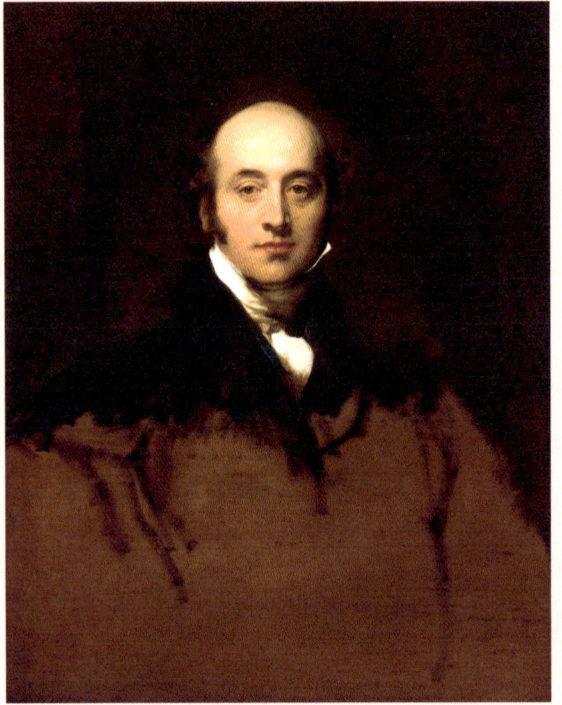

Benjamin West PRA, *Self-portrait*, 1793

Sir Thomas Lawrence PRA, *Self-portrait*, *c.* 1825

been identified as republican in his political leanings. His death in 1820, shortly after George III, brought about the election as President of the brilliant portrait painter Sir Thomas Lawrence.

Lawrence, who had studied at the Royal Academy Schools, was elected an Associate Royal Academician before he was 25. Renowned for the society portraits he showed at the Annual Exhibition, he was well liked by the new King, George IV, who presented him with a heavy gold medal that is still worn by the President today. Giampietrino's near-contemporary copy of Leonardo's *Last Supper* – a work used for teaching in the Royal Academy Schools, and more recently as an invaluable reference during restoration of the original at Santa Maria delle Grazie in Milan – was purchased on Lawrence's instructions in 1821. Despite his success, Lawrence's obsessive collecting left him frequently short of money. He died in 1830, shortly before George IV, and was buried at St Paul's Cathedral, near Reynolds and West. Turner painted the ceremony.

It was in 1830, too, that Michelangelo's *Virgin and Child with the Infant St John*, the so-called Taddei Tondo of *c.* 1504–05, was presented to the Academy by descendants of Sir George Beaumont. Beaumont was a patron of Constable and an art collector who did much to establish the National Gallery and its magnificent collection of pictures. The tondo, Michelangelo's only marble sculpture in Britain, had been owned by the Florentine Taddei family for centuries before being purchased in Rome by Beaumont. It is unquestionably the Academy's greatest treasure, and is greatly admired for the forceful attack of its chisel work.

In 1830 the Royal Academicians elected the Irish portrait painter Sir Martin Archer Shee to succeed Lawrence as their President. A talented draughtsman in his childhood, Shee had attended the Royal Academy Schools and was quickly elected a Royal Academician. His twenty years in the presidency provided the Academy with a strong advocate in the face of a period of severe criticism and government scrutiny. This culminated in the institution vacating New Somerset House, its premises needed for the growing departments of the civil service. The Academy's next home was to be a grand new edifice in Trafalgar Square.

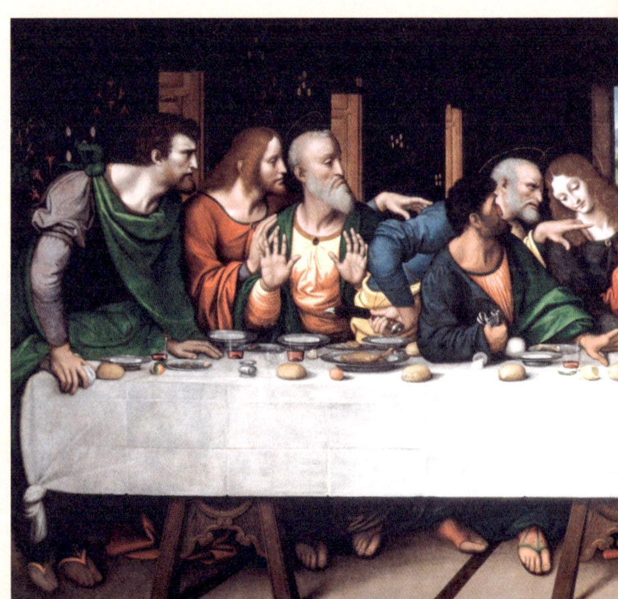

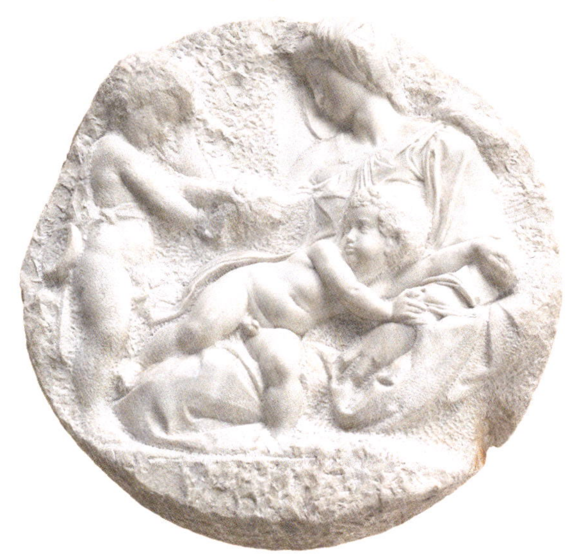

Michelangelo Buonarroti, *The Virgin and Child with the Infant St John*, the Taddei Tondo, *c.* 1504–05

Giampietrino, after Leonardo da Vinci, *The Last Supper*, *c.* 1520

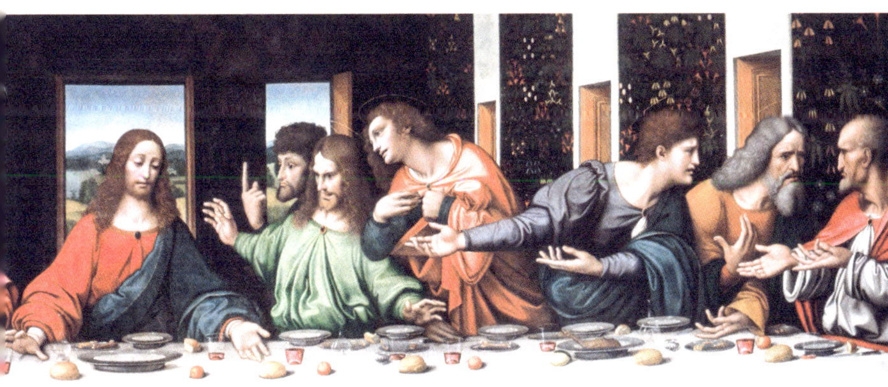

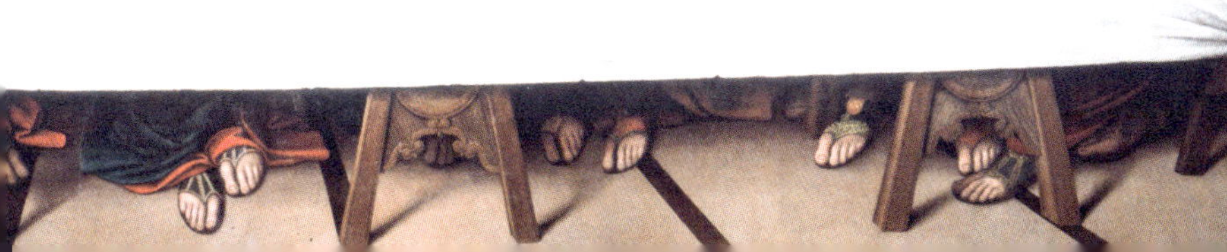

TRAFALGAR SQUARE

1837–67

In April 1837 King William IV opened a palatial new building overlooking Trafalgar Square. This was to be shared accommodation for the National Gallery and the Royal Academy. The National Gallery had been formed around the picture collection of John Julius Angerstein, purchased from his estate by the Government in 1824 (a purchase that Sir Thomas Lawrence PRA had encouraged). The pictures were initially displayed at Angerstein's house in Pall Mall, but the spaces there were domestic and it was soon clear that a new building would be needed. After much debate, Trafalgar Square was selected as the optimum location, on the site of William Kent's King's Mews and midway between the fashionable West End and the less prosperous areas to the east, thus enabling all members of society to congregate and view their collection of pictures. At one point John Nash considered a separate building for the Academy, to be based on the Parthenon, to stand in front of a building for the National Gallery, but in the end the Royal Academician William Wilkins won the day.

There were compromises from the outset. Wilkins was obliged to build one room deep, as behind his site stood a barracks and a workhouse. His façade had to be set back further than he wished to prevent interference with the view of St Martin-in-the-Fields. The ground and principal floors of Wilkins's east wing were apportioned to the Royal Academy, with the National Gallery to the west. Proximity to the National Gallery's

Old Masters was an undoubted advantage for students of the Royal Academy Schools, but there were frustrations too: during the Annual Exhibition, the Professors, Visitors and students could not use many of the teaching rooms, which were used for hanging the show; each year, indeed, the Academy's Life School had to move to the drum of the building's central dome, whose tall arched windows, invisible from Trafalgar Square, provided north light.

Mason Jackson, *Taking in the Pictures at the RA*, April 1866

William Payne, *Private View of the Royal Academy*, 1858

Overleaf: William Wilkins RA, *The Galleries and Ground Floor of the National Gallery, Trafalgar Square*, 1836

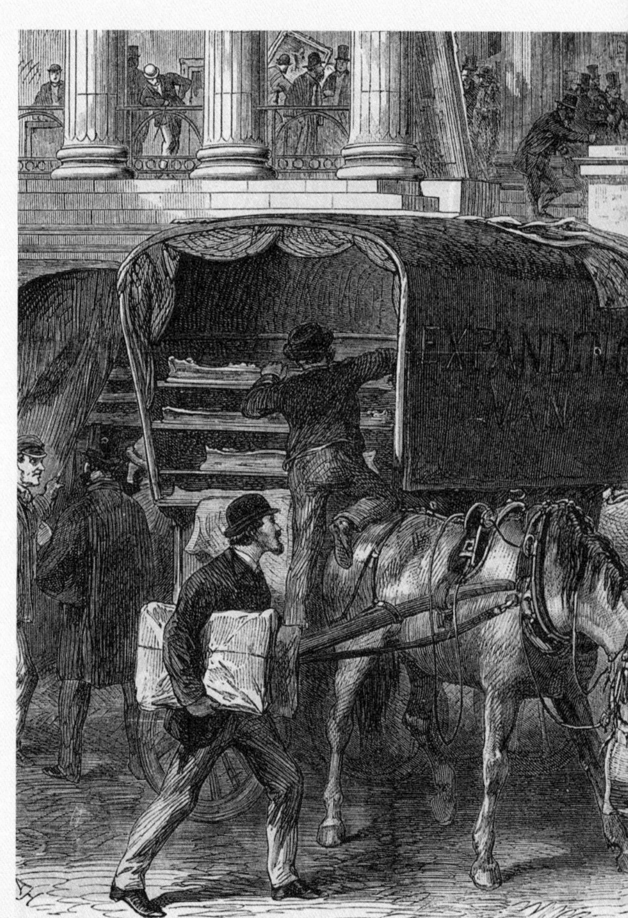

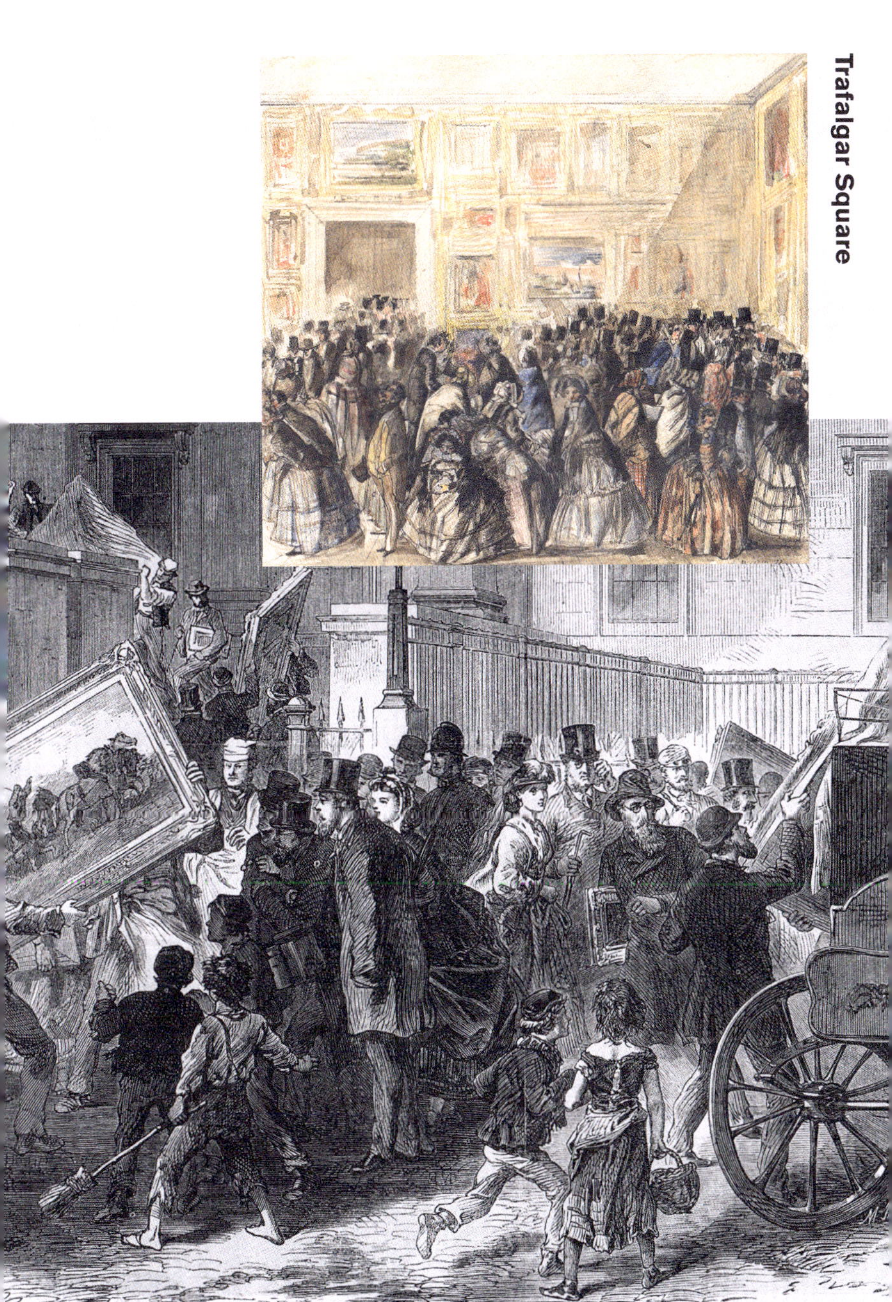

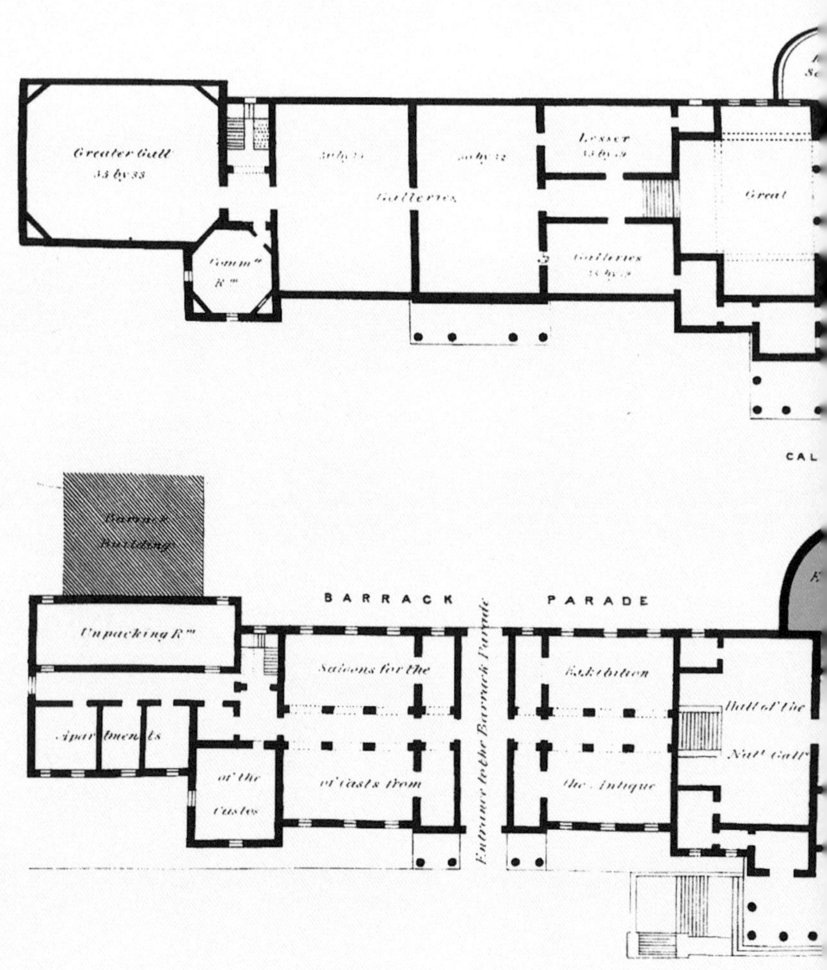

Greater Gall
33 by 33
Galleries
Lesser
Great
Galleries
Barrack
Building
BARRACK
PARADE
Unpacking Rm
Saloons for the
of casts from
Exhibition
the Antique
Entrance to the Barrack Parade
Hall of the
Apartments
of the

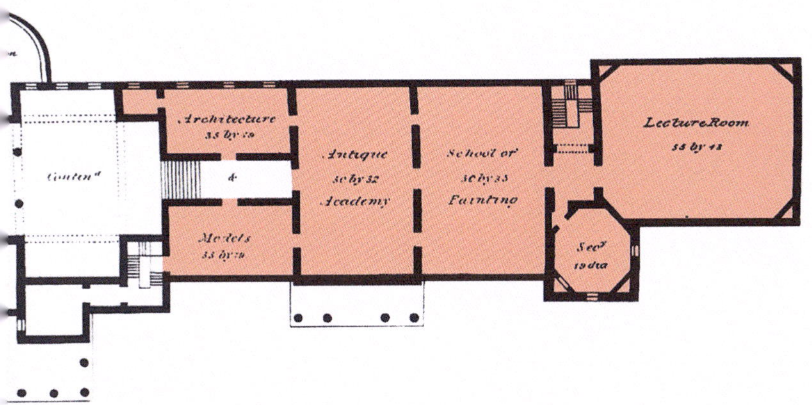

LOOR

N. B.—The part coloured Red is appropriated to the **Royal Academy.**

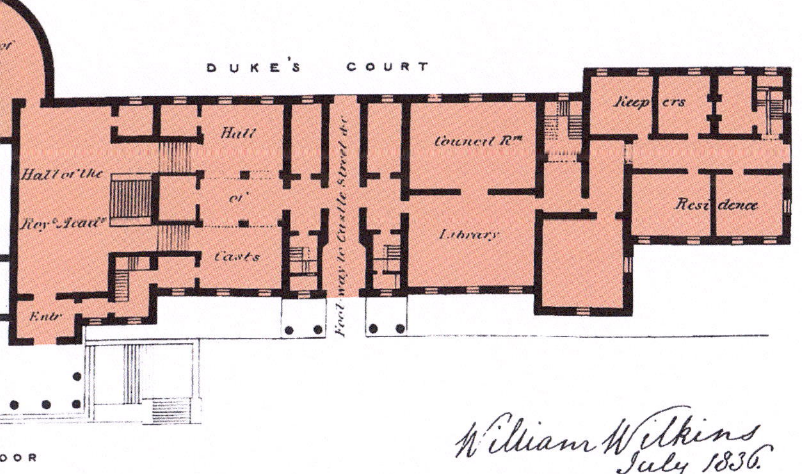

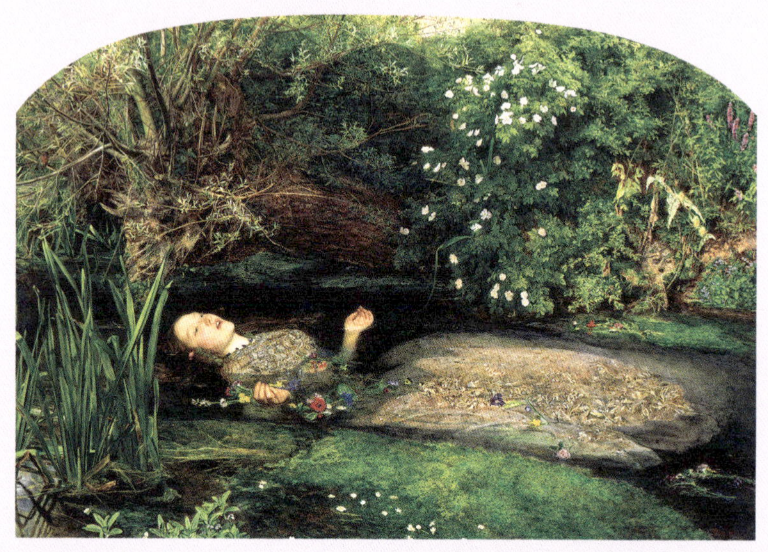

Sir John Everett Millais Bt PRA, *Ophelia*, 1851–52

Sir John Everett Millais Bt PRA, *John Ruskin*, 1853–54

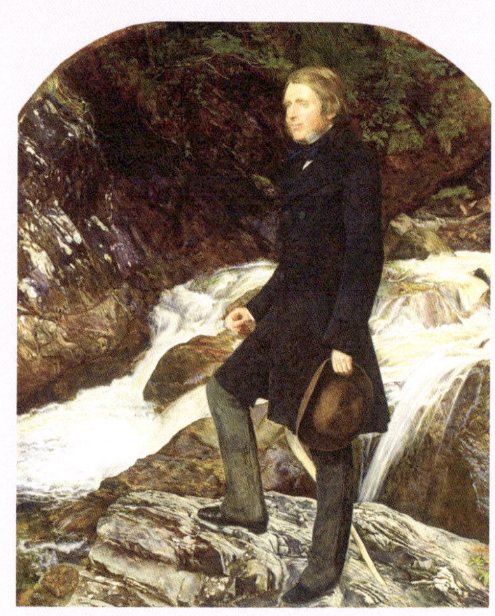

Shee was a trustee of the National Gallery, as was his successor as President of the Royal Academy, Sir Charles Lock Eastlake, whom the Academicians elected in 1850. Eastlake pulled off the not inconsiderable feat of combining the role with directorship of the National Gallery. He must have found himself under constant pressure from both institutions: the National Gallery had almost doubled the size of its holdings since its foundation, having received Turner's great bequest of pictures in the early 1850s; and the Academy's Annual Exhibition was receiving ever-increasing numbers of entries.

John Ruskin, an early supporter of the initially unpopular Pre-Raphaelite Brotherhood, wrote annual critiques of the works in the Royal Academy Exhibitions for some of these years. These were keenly scrutinised by collectors and artists, whose fortunes could rise and fall by them. The satirical magazine *Punch* even published a comic verse on the subject:

I paints and paints,
hears no complaints
And sells before I'm dry,
Till savage Ruskin
He sticks his tusk in
Then nobody will buy.

BURLINGTON HOUSE

1868–

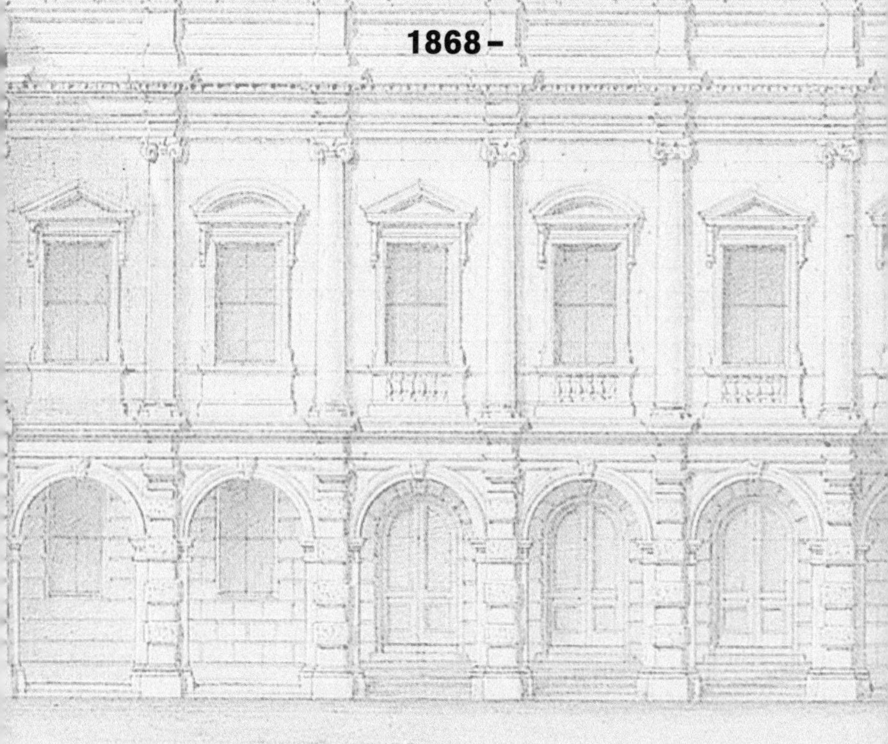

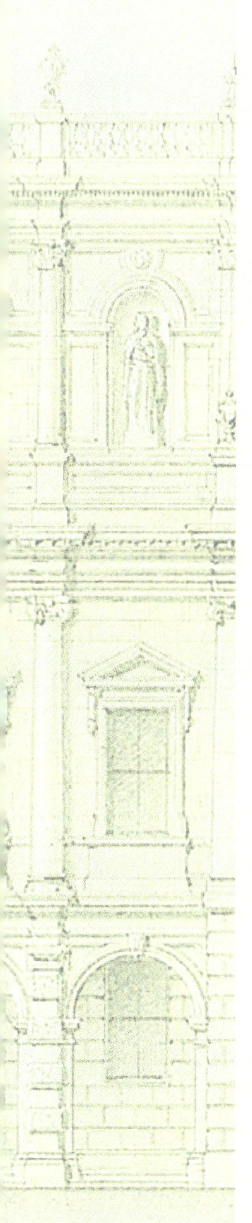

Eastlake's time in charge coincided with a period of parliamentary scrutiny of the Academy and its activities in the form of a Royal Commission, which criticism the President and his Royal Academicians handled well. At one point it looked as though the National Gallery might choose to leave Trafalgar Square for South Kensington or Burlington House, Piccadilly, but eventually the Government decided that the National Gallery should take over the Academy's spaces at Trafalgar Square. Eastlake made it clear that equivalent premises would have to be provided for the Royal Academicians to make good the exchange. Queen Victoria was on the lookout for additional adornments to her project to memorialise her husband on the South Kensington estate that had been developed with the proceeds of the Great Exhibition, which Prince Albert had overseen in 1851. But the Academicians, always independent-minded in their approach, felt that Kensington was too distant from central London. In the end, they moved to Burlington House, where their new President from 1866, the painter Sir Francis Grant, secured the institution's tenure of its new home on exceptionally favourable terms: an annual rent of £1 for 999 years. In return, the Academicians undertook to build and maintain at their own expense an additional storey on top of Lord Burlington's house, and a set of exhibition galleries and a series of studios for the Royal Academy Schools on the house's large rear gardens.

By the time the Academy arrived in Piccadilly

in 1868, Burlington House already had a long and distinguished history. Built in the seventeenth century for Sir John Denham, the house had been purchased incomplete by a forebear of Richard Boyle, 3rd Earl of Burlington. Burlington inherited it in 1704, and it was remodelled during his minority, probably to designs by James Gibbs. After his Grand Tour, Burlington instructed Colen Campbell to alter the façade. While in Italy, Burlington had become an advocate for the classical style of architecture that had been perfected by Andrea Palladio in Venice and the Veneto in the sixteenth century, and his use of this Palladian style at Burlington House and later at Chiswick House helped greatly to establish it as an integral part of Britain's architectural vocabulary. In the courtyard before the house, James Gibbs's baroque colonnades met at Colen Campbell's great arched gateway onto Piccadilly. Lord Burlington engaged William Kent to decorate the state rooms of his house, and the spirit of his interiors survives, as do some of the series of large mythological paintings that Sebastiano Ricci made for the staircase and its ceiling. Kent lived at Burlington House until his death in 1748, and must often have encountered Lord Burlington's other artistic protégés Alexander Pope and George Frideric Handel there.

After Burlington's day, ownership of the house passed through the hands of members of his family. One of these, Lord George Cavendish, installed the great central staircase, which is now so familiar to visitors, having later been extended upwards

Sir Francis Grant PRA, *Self-portrait*, 1876

Johannes Kip, after Leonard Knyff, *Burlington House in Pickadilly*, from *Britannia Illustrata, London*, 1707, plate 29

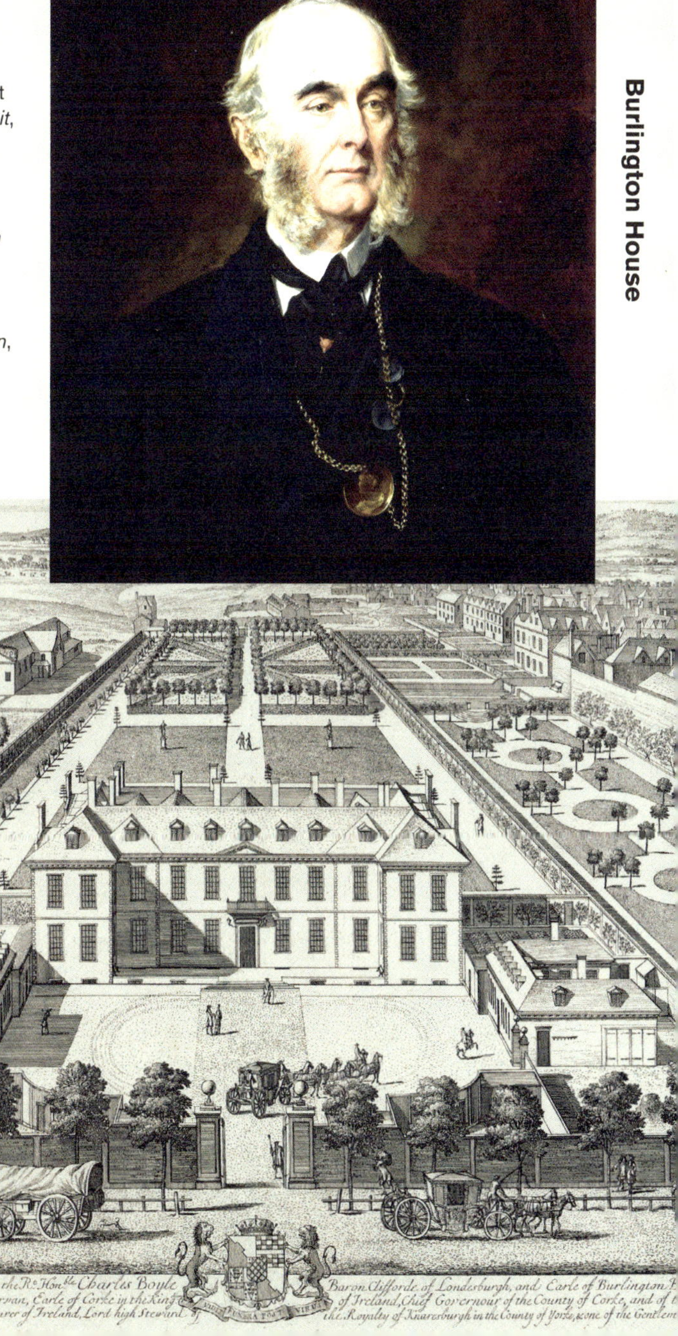

William Aikman, *William Kent*, c. 1723–25

Elevated view of Burlington House, Piccadilly, 1866. Wood engraving from the *Illustrated London News*, 15 September 1866

The Saloon, Burlington House, looking east through the enfilade. The Fine Rooms were restored in 2004 through the generosity of John Madejski

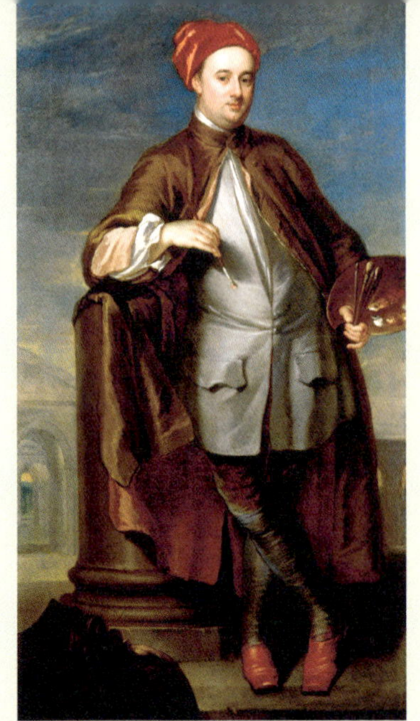

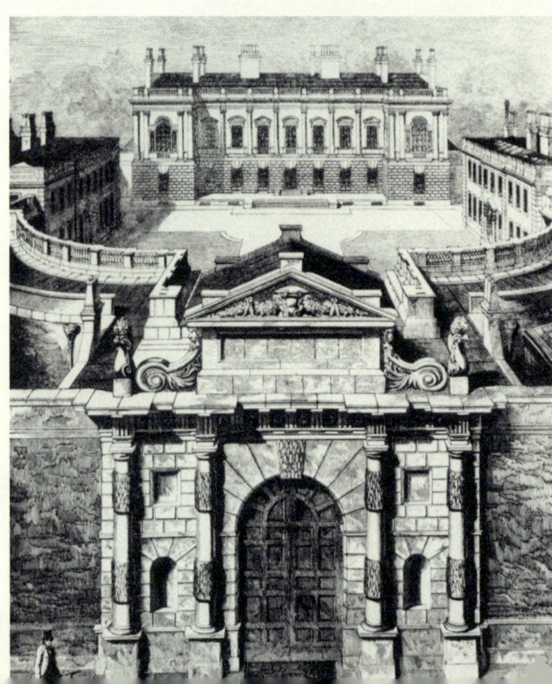

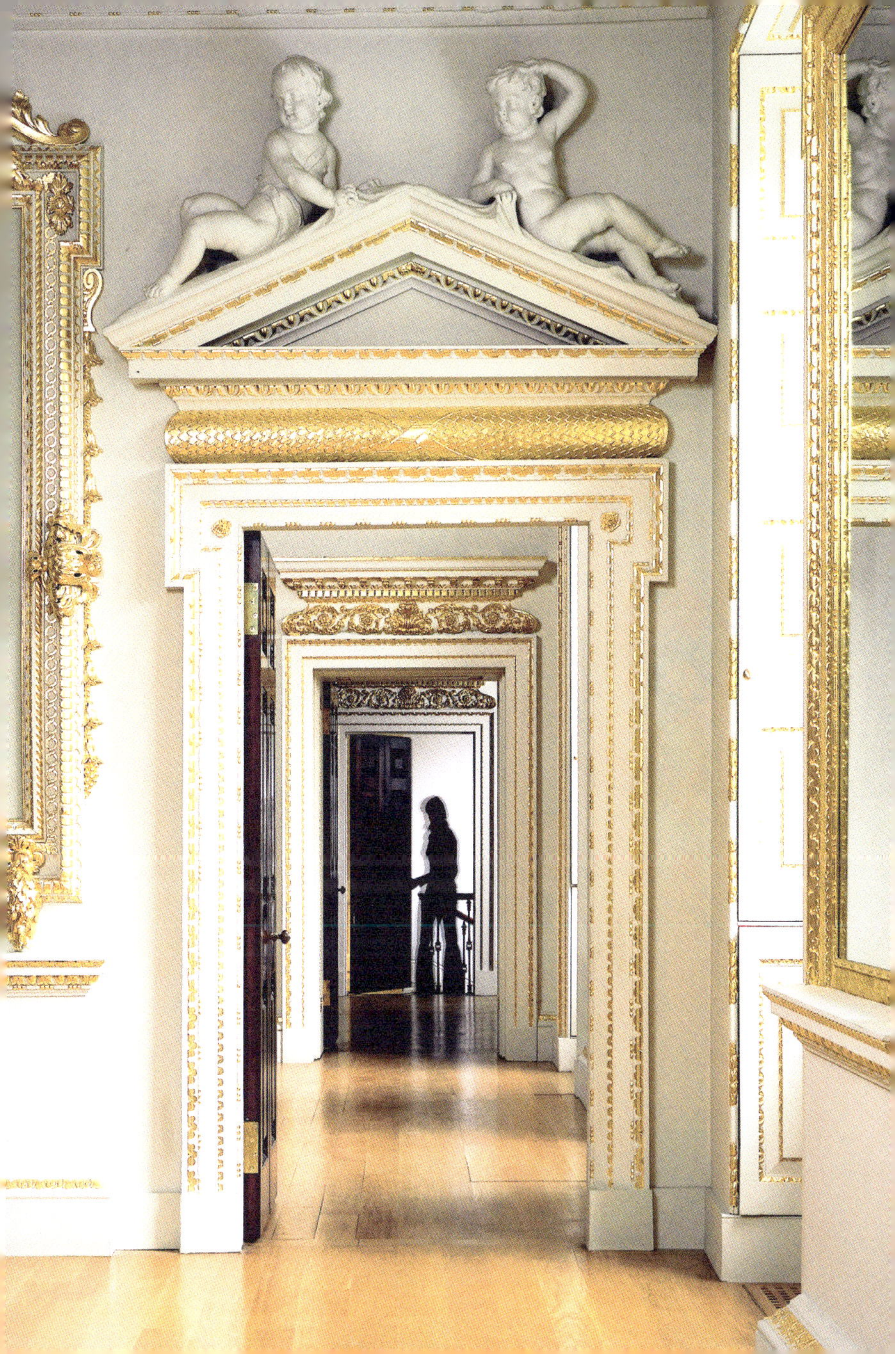

towards the Academy's new galleries. Burlington House was eventually purchased by the Government, and its flanking service wings, colonnades and arch demolished by the Victorians to permit the construction of the Venetian-inspired buildings by the firm of Banks and Barry that surround today's Annenberg Courtyard. These courtyard buildings house five learned societies: the Royal Society of Chemistry, the Geological Society of London, the Royal Astronomical Society, the Linnean Society of London, and the Society of Antiquaries of London.

At the same time, the architect Sydney Smirke, the Academy's Treasurer, added an upper storey to Campbell's Palladian façade to house a suite of smaller galleries, funded mainly by a generous bequest from the successful sculptor-Academician John Gibson. These housed a display of Gibson's works and the Academicians' Diploma Works, causing them to become known as the Diploma Galleries. Statues in niches on the storey's exterior depict Phidias, Leonardo, Flaxman, Raphael, Michelangelo, Titian, Reynolds, Wren and Bishop William of Wykeham: note the neat equivalence between Greek and Italian artistic titans and British masters and patrons.

Behind Burlington House, on its gardens, the Royal Academy built a spectacular set of top-lit galleries to designs again by Smirke, who had worked with his brother Robert on the design of the great domed Reading Room at the British Museum. Smirke's symmetrical floorplan is centred on an

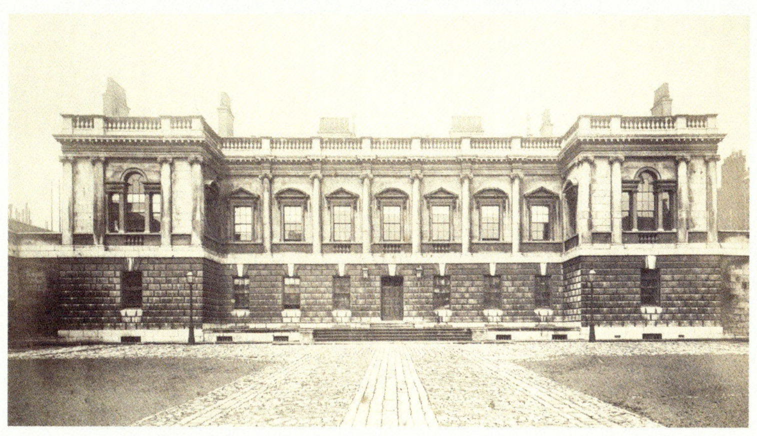

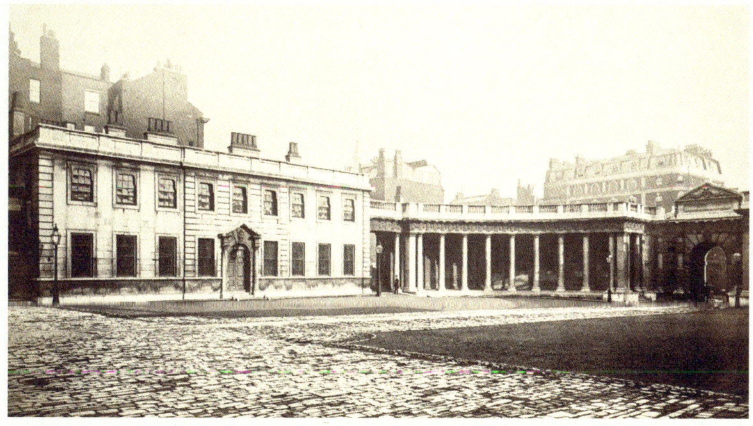

These nineteenth-century photographs by Stephen Ayling show Burlington House before the arrival of the Royal Academy: top, the south front, and above, one of the flanking service wings, Gibbs's colonnade and Campbell's arched gateway to Piccadilly

Overleaf: the interior of Gallery III by Sydney Smirke RA, the Royal Academy's largest exhibition room

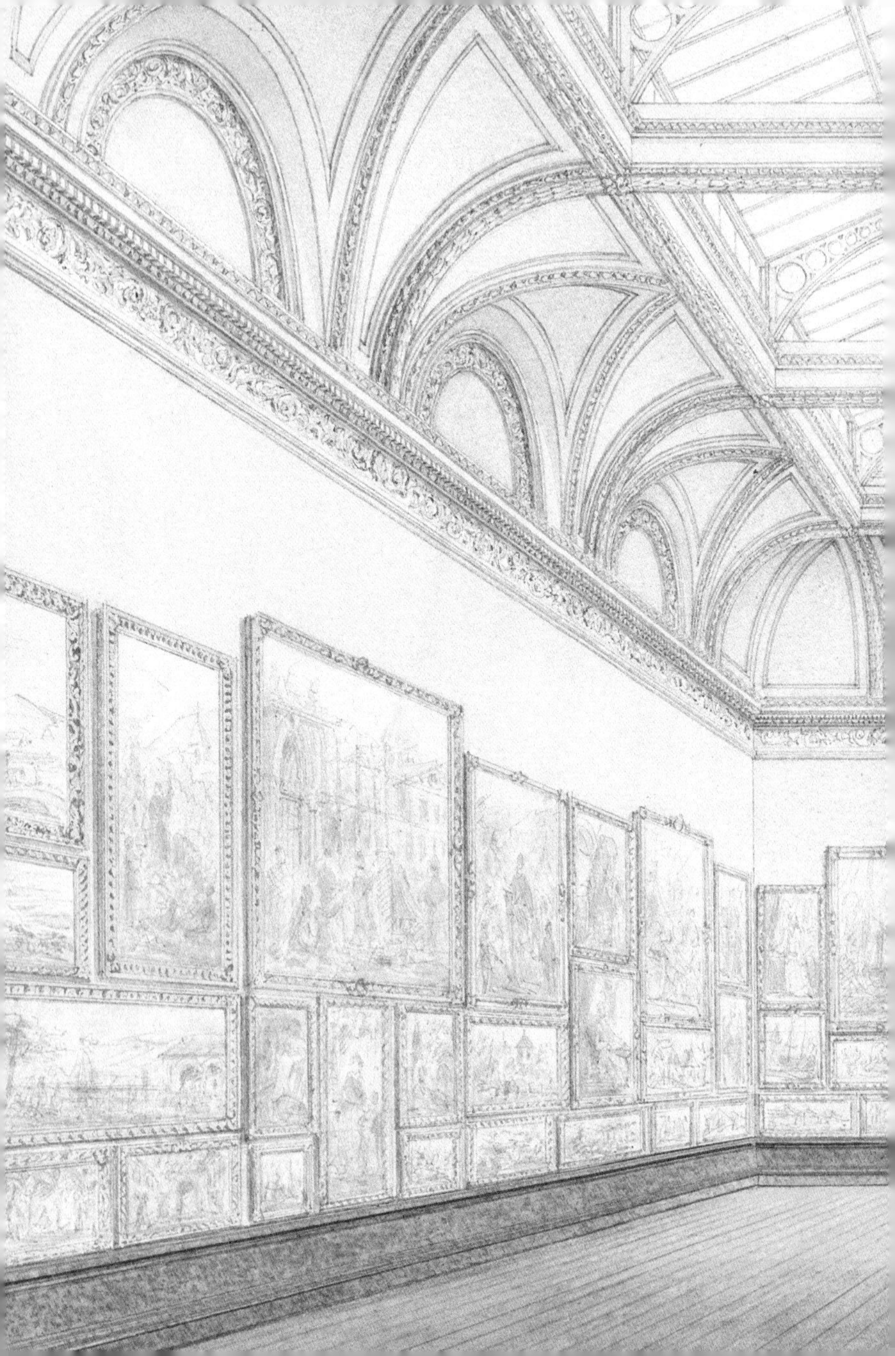

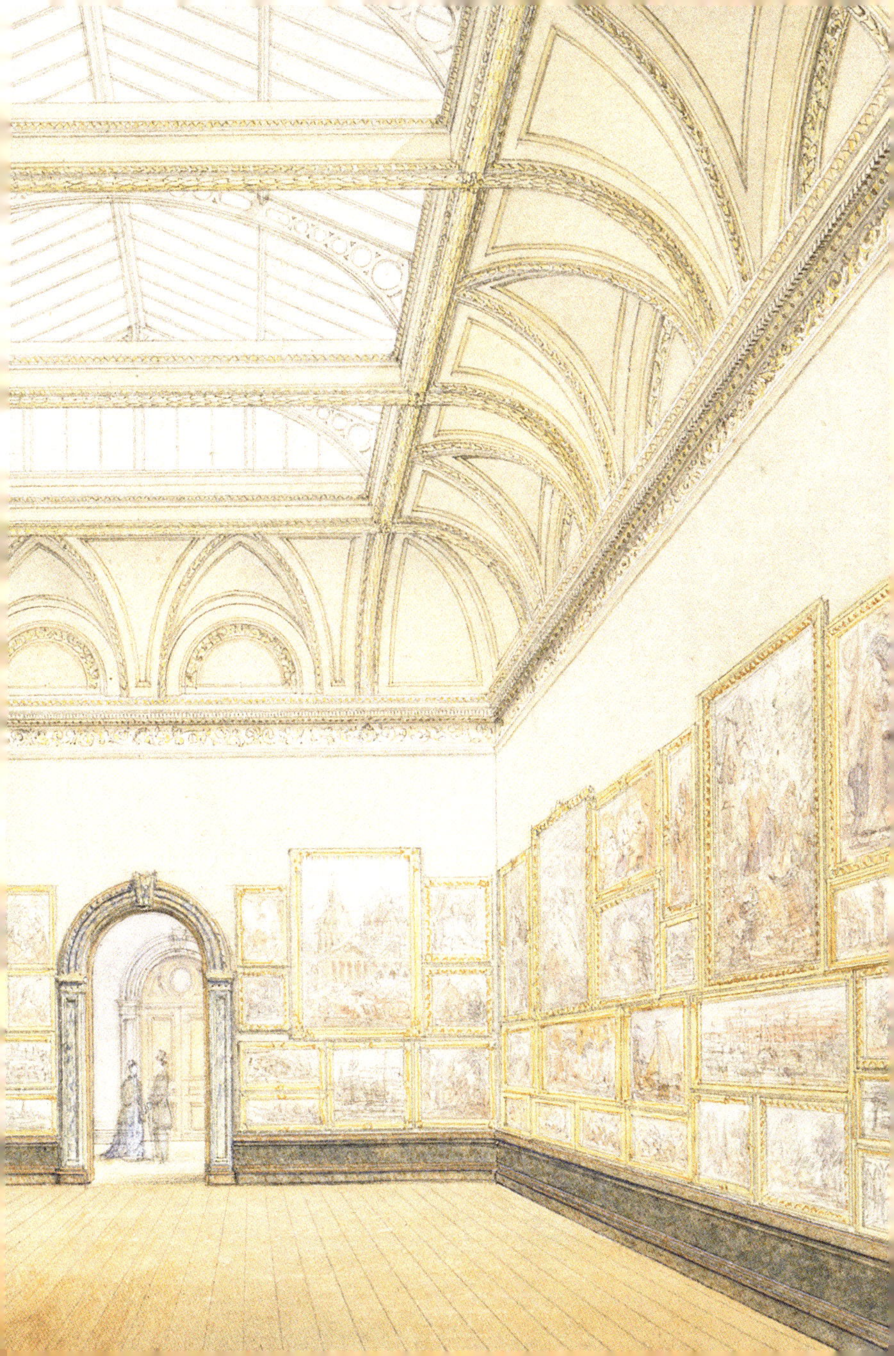

octagonal central hall, offering axial vistas in each direction. From gilded roundels, busts of Italian and British artists look down and again remind visitors of the status of the arts in this country. Gallery III, the most expansive of Smirke's handsome rooms and the focal point of the Summer Exhibition, is perhaps the nineteenth century's answer to the eighteenth century's Great Room at New Somerset House. Astonishingly, construction of these new galleries took barely twelve months. The rich variety of classical ornament and the liberal use of gold leaf in the coved ceilings are signs of the confidence and wealth of the era that produced them.

The Academy's creation of these new galleries was a masterstroke, providing the Academicians with a lucid and rational set of spaces for the Summer Exhibition, as it gradually came to be known after the move to Burlington House, and, from 1870, for the so-called Winter Exhibitions. These displays of works of art lent by private collectors, and later by whole countries, were an important new strand in the Academy's activities, and are the precursors of today's international loan exhibitions.

So the scene was set for the late nineteenth-century Academy, the institution that more than any other stood at the centre of the High Victorian art world. One picture that opens a window onto those 'palmy days', to quote a former Secretary, Sidney C. Hutchison, is Charles West Cope's depiction of the Academicians in their magnificent new galleries during the selection process for the

Charles West Cope RA, *The Council of the Royal Academy Selecting Pictures for the Exhibition, 1875*, 1876

Summer Exhibition of 1875. Grant sits in the President's chair, holding the gavel that symbolises the assembled Academicians' judgement on each picture, while a group of art handlers await their verdict, to be chalked on the stretcher: 'A' for Accepted, 'D' for Doubtful, 'R' for Rejected. Frederic Leighton sits two to Grant's right, with John Everett Millais in the foreground; two Presidents in waiting. Cope captures the excitement of the installation of the Summer Exhibition and the heady atmosphere that must have characterised the Academy's first years in Piccadilly. With such lofty and spacious rooms, the size and quantity of works selected increased, as did visitor numbers.

The Royal Academy Schools benefited greatly from the move, too. Designed by Smirke and then

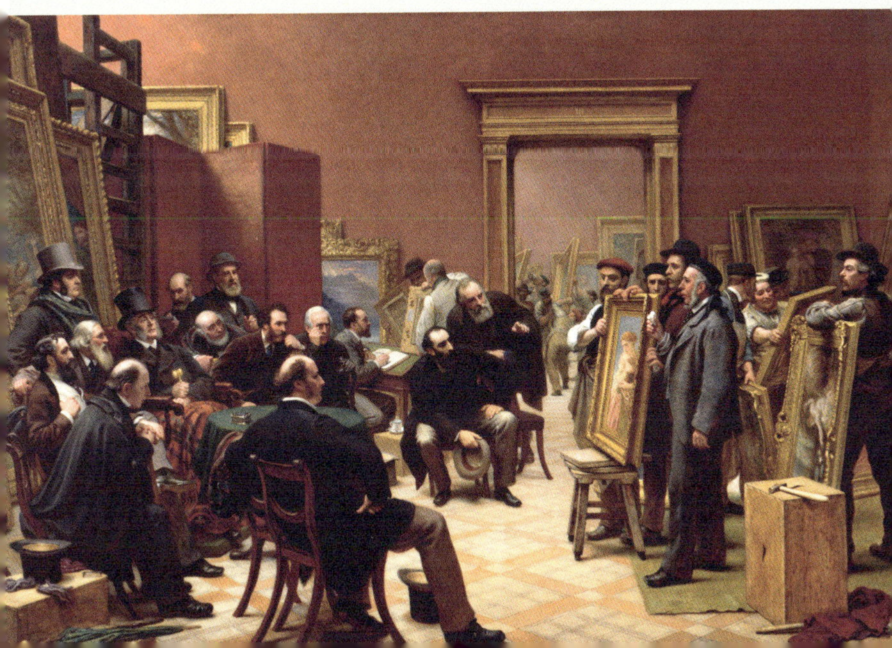

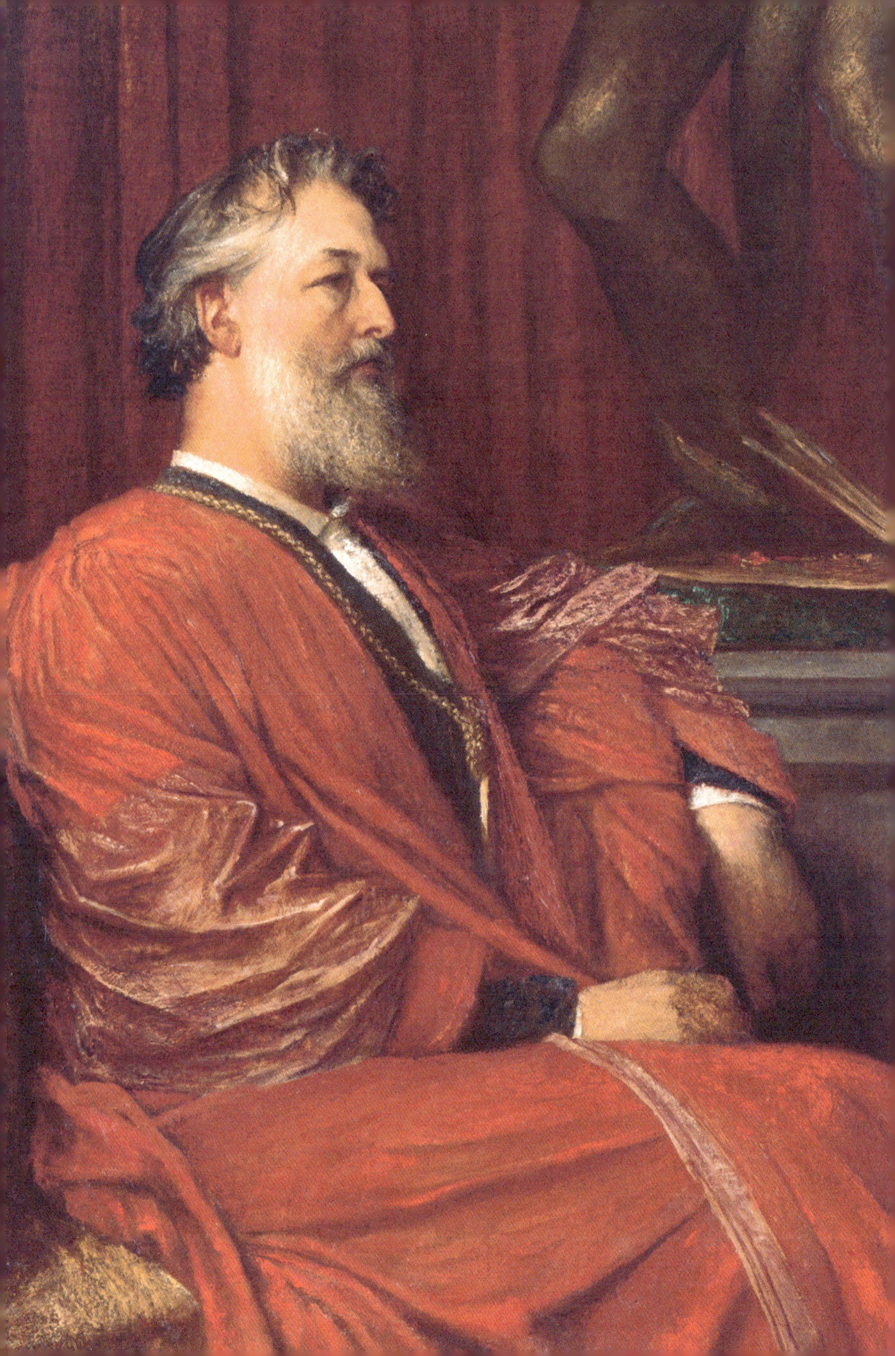

George Frederic Watts RA, *Frederic, Lord Leighton PRA*, 1888

Richard Norman Shaw, their new studios, top-lit with north light, and opening off a fine vaulted and cast-lined corridor running beneath Smirke's new galleries, faced the rising rear elevation of a large new building for the University of London by Sir James Pennethorne, which was eventually to belong to the Academy. At last, students could work in the Schools without having to move out during the Summer Exhibition.

When Grant died in 1878, he was succeeded in the presidency by Frederic Leighton. A sculptor and painter, Leighton was something of a polymath, and a prodigious traveller. The first work he showed at the Annual Exhibition, in 1855, was purchased by Queen Victoria, and thereafter his success was assured. With its magnificently tiled Arab Hall, his house in Holland Park, like the many other painters' studio-homes nearby and in St John's Wood, is testament to the wealth and status to which nineteenth-century artists could aspire, thanks in large part to the prominence that membership of the Royal Academy gave them.

William Powell Frith's *A Private View at the Royal Academy, 1881* gives an impression of the significance of the opening of the Summer Exhibition within Victorian metropolitan society. Anthony Trollope, William Gladstone, Ellen Terry, Lillie Langtry and Oscar Wilde, wearing a buttonhole, have all been identified among the crowds. A powerful force in the Academy, Leighton exerted a benign influence over submissions to the Summer

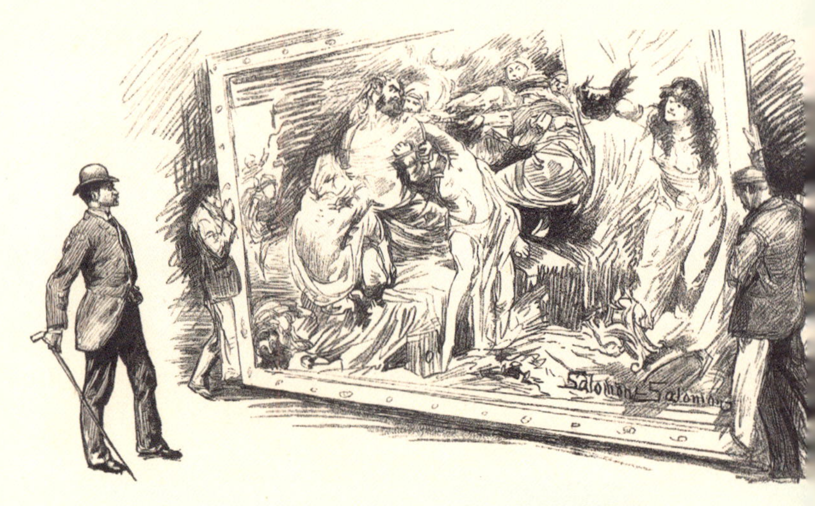
Salomon Salomon

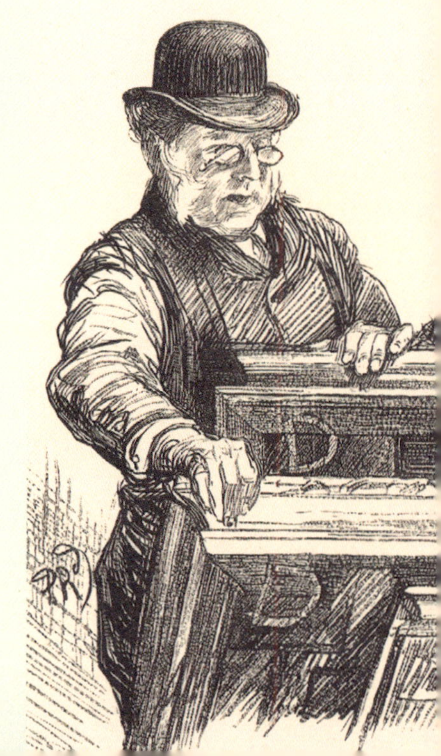

The Royal Academy. Wood engravings after Charles Paul Renouard, published in *The Graphic*, 1887

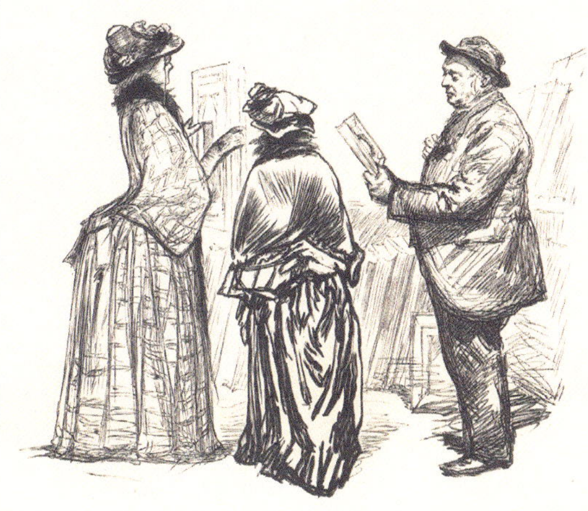

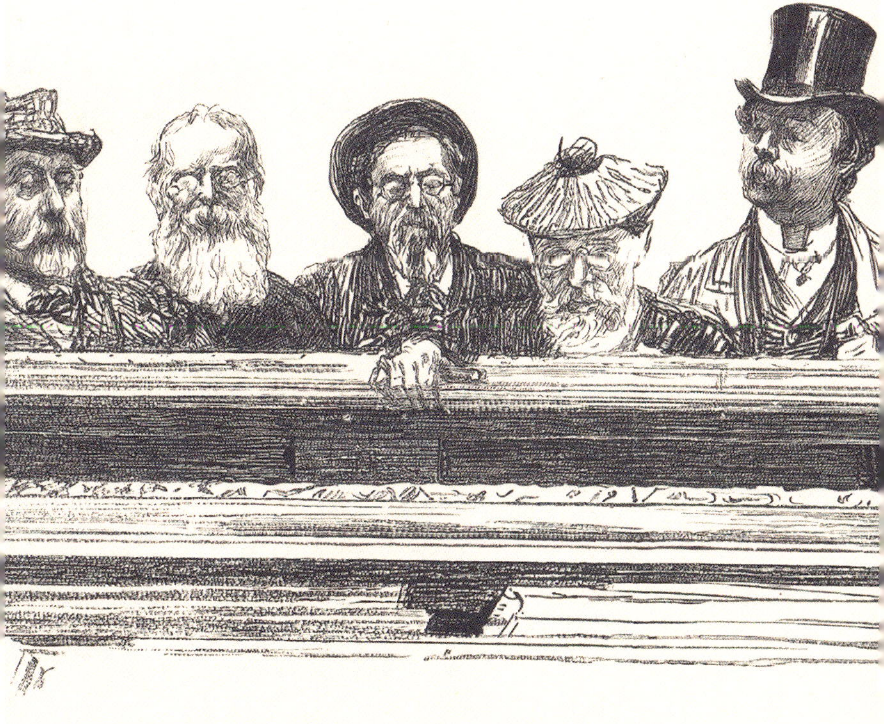

Exhibition and over the activities of the Royal Academy Schools. His advancement of sculpture led to the rise of the movement known as the New Sculpture. When he died in 1896, his friend and supporter the painter Sir John Everett Millais Bt was elected in his place, but died himself soon afterwards.

The loss of two such artistic giants in close succession was a blow. Sir Edward Poynter Bt, who was elected PRA to succeed Millais in 1896, painted scenes of everyday life in the ancient world. Like Eastlake, he combined the presidency with directorship of the National Gallery for a time, and witnessed from Burlington House the periods of mourning for both Queen Victoria and King Edward VII.

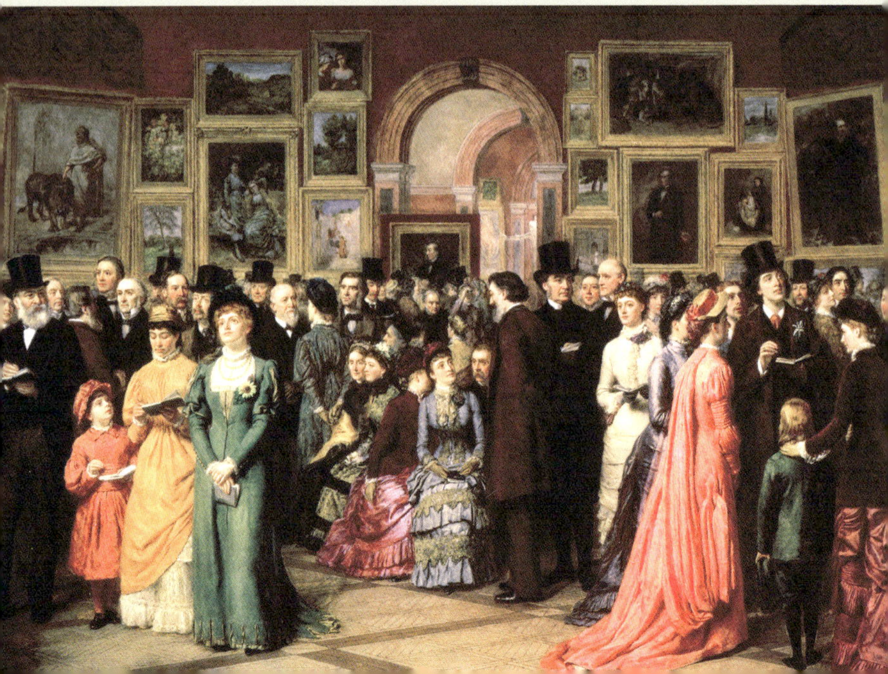

William Powell Frith RA, *A Private View at the Royal Academy, 1881*, 1883

Sir Hamo Thornycroft RA, *Teucer*, 1881

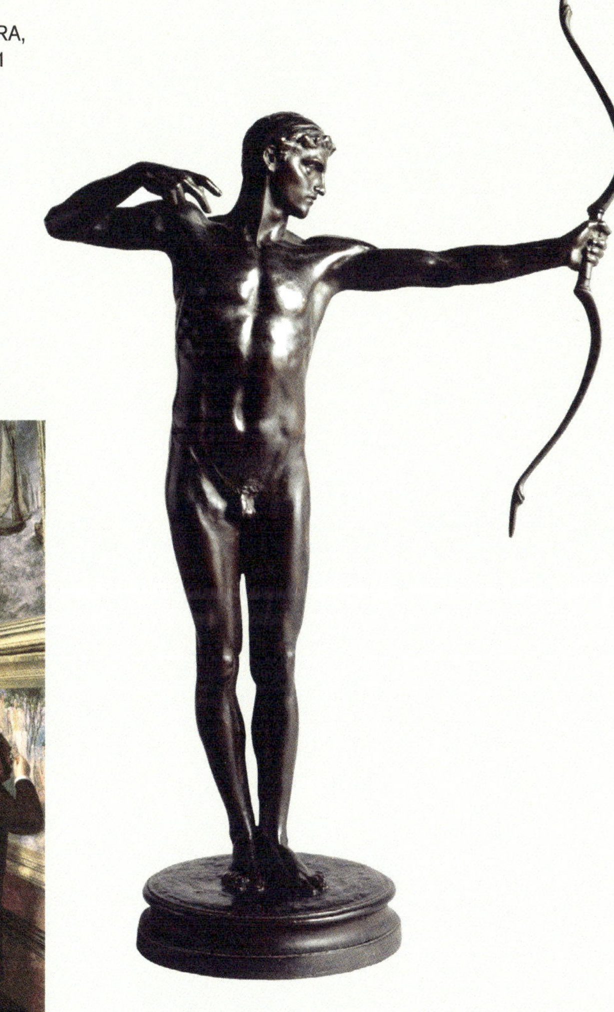

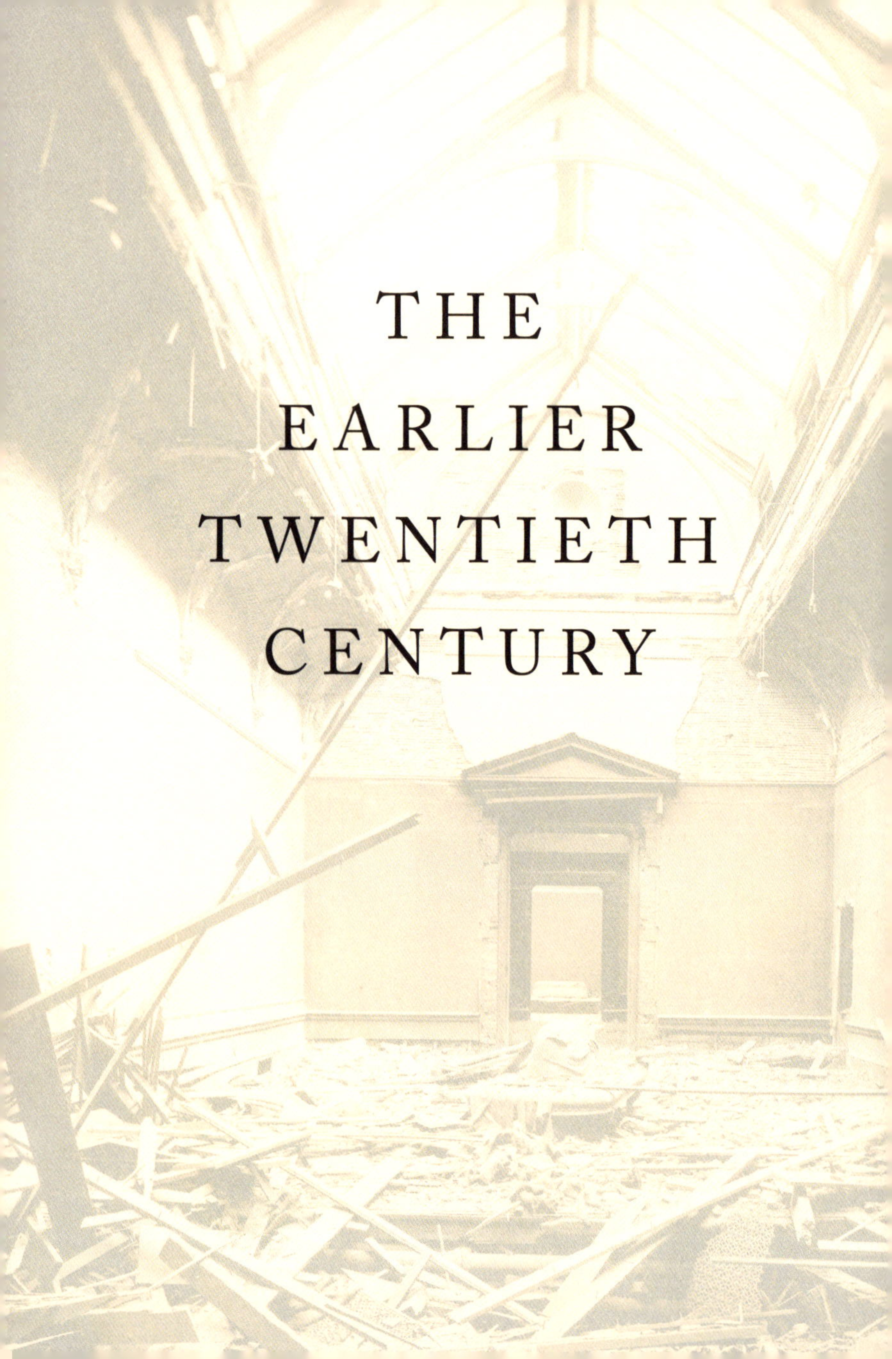

THE EARLIER TWENTIETH CENTURY

British society underwent profound change in the new century. In the Summer Exhibition of 1914, just before the outbreak of the First World War, John Singer Sargent's portrait of the American novelist Henry James and a nude by Sir George Clausen were slashed by protesting suffragettes. During the war the Summer Exhibitions continued, although without celebratory openings, and the Royal Academy Schools housed a unit that designed camouflage for naval ships. One of Smirke's galleries was badly damaged by a bomb.

At the end of the war Poynter resigned and was succeeded as PRA in 1919 by Sir Aston Webb, architect of the Mall façade of Buckingham Palace. Attendances at the Summer Exhibitions gradually returned to their pre-war levels, and a large loan exhibition of Spanish art took place, the first of a series of shows of national art collections to visit Burlington House. Sir Frank Dicksee succeeded Webb as PRA in 1924, the majority of Academicians feeling that they should next elect a painter and not another architect, although Sir Reginald Blomfield had been the favourite of many. Dicksee was always busy in his studio, at work on mythical and legendary subjects. On his death in 1928, the Welsh painter Sir William Llewellyn was elected PRA to succeed him.

It was at this time that the Academy's loan exhibitions of national treasures really came into their own, with a show of Dutch art dating from 1450 to 1900. The Italian exhibition that followed in 1930, under the auspices of the dictator Benito

TRAVEL L.N.E.R

ROYAL ACADEMY OF ARTS
PICCADILLY LONDON

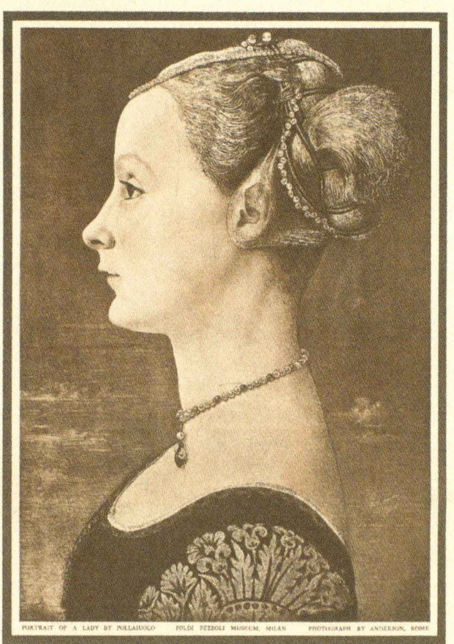

PORTRAIT OF A LADY BY POLLAIUOLO   POLDI PEZZOLI MUSEUM, MILAN   PHOTOGRAPH BY ANDERSON, ROME

EXHIBITION OF
ITALIAN ART

1200–1900

1 JAN. TO 8 MAR. 1930

MONDAY TO SATURDAY 9.30–7

ADMISSION 1/6 FRIDAYS 5/-

Season Tickets 10/6 from the Secretary-General 117 Victoria St. S.W.1

Mussolini, comprised works dating from 1200 to 1900. Some 1,000 exhibits travelled by sea, their vessel especially renamed the *Leonardo da Vinci* for the purpose. Among them were such treasures as Botticelli's *Birth of Venus* from Florence, Mantegna's *Lamentation over the Dead Christ* from Milan and Giorgione's *La Tempesta* from Venice. Some 600,000 attended, and long queues stretched across the courtyard. During preparations for the Persian exhibition in 1931 some works were found to have

Sponsored by Mussolini, the 'Exhibition of Italian Art' (1930) brought masterpieces of the Italian Renaissance to Burlington House

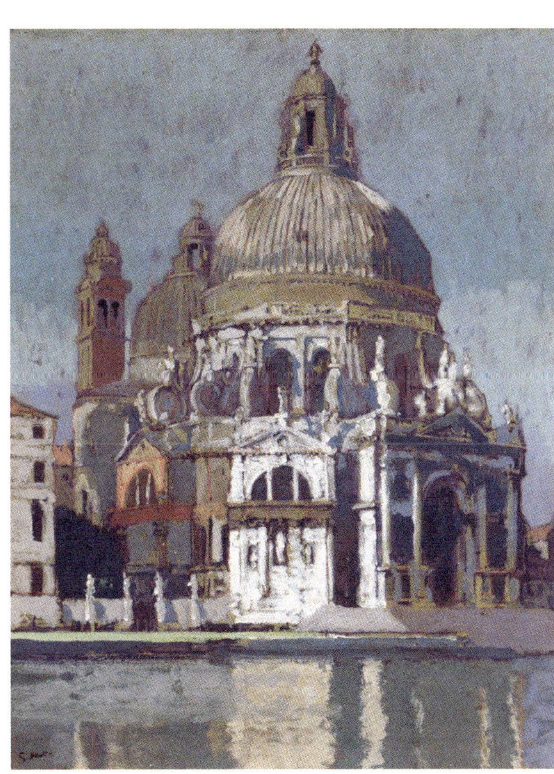

Walter Sickert RA, *Santa Maria della Salute*, c. 1901

Wyndham Lewis, *T. S. Eliot*, 1938

Robert Lutyens, *Sir Edwin Lutyens*, 1959

Sir Alfred Munnings, 1957–58

been packed in camel dung. French art from 1200 to 1900 was the subject of 1932's show, British art from 1000 to 1860 in 1934, and Chinese art in 1935–36.

There was a spate of resignations in these years: Stanley Spencer, over the hang of his works in the Summer Exhibition in 1935; Walter Sickert, angry with Llewellyn for his failure to support Jacob Epstein, whose sculpted figures on the façade of a building in the Strand were threatened by new tenants; and Augustus John, fuming about the rejection from the 1938 Summer Exhibition of Wyndham Lewis's portrait of T. S. Eliot.

The turn of another architect came in the election of Sir Edwin Lutyens as PRA in 1938. Clubbable,

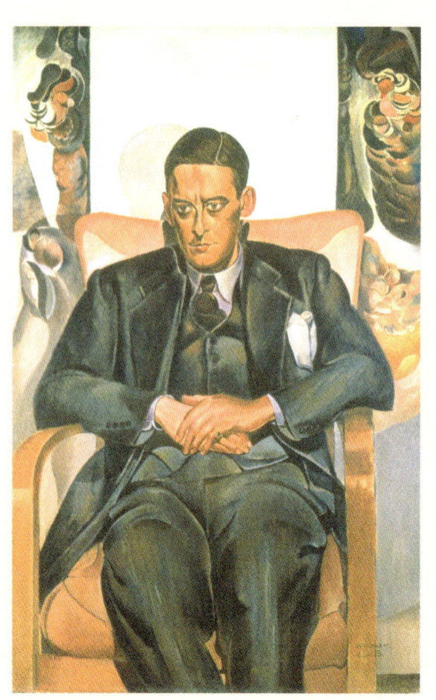

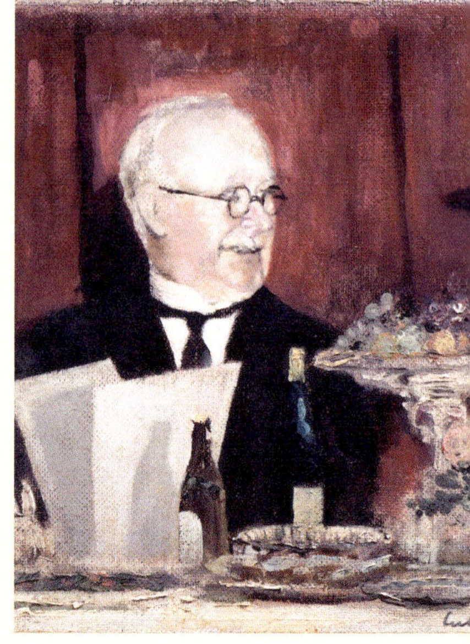

successful and witty, Lutyens is best known for his domestic architecture and for having designed the Cenotaph in Whitehall and the majestic Viceroy's House and government buildings at New Delhi. Few celebrations were held during his presidency, which coincided with the privations of the Second World War, although impressively the Summer Exhibition continued throughout.

On Lutyens's death in 1944, the Academicians elected Alfred Munnings as their President. Munnings was an exceptionally fine painter, especially of horses, but he had an uneasy relationship with the avant-garde throughout his career. In his last year in office, in his cups,

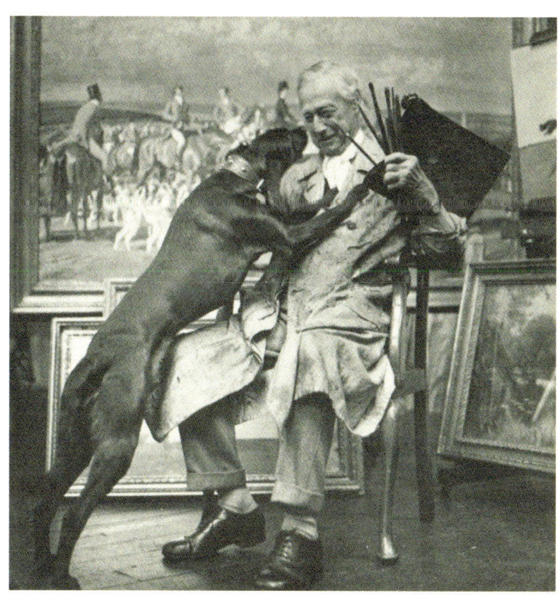

Leonardo da Vinci, *The Virgin and Child with St Anne and St John the Baptist*, *c.* 1499–1500

he made a speech at the Annual Dinner, which at that time was broadcast live on the BBC's Home Service, during which he attempted to enlist Sir Winston Churchill, himself a painter and an honoured guest at the dinner, in support of his views on the art of Matisse and Picasso. Churchill, embarrassed, wrote to 'protest … against these utterances'. Munnings's extempore words cast a long shadow, and several decades were to pass before the Academy recovered its reputation for openness.

During the presidencies of the renowned portrait painter Sir Gerald Kelly (1949–54), the architect Sir Albert Richardson (1954–56), who, nostalgic for the Georgian era, delighted in denigrating modern buildings, and Sir Charles Wheeler (1956–66), the first sculptor to be elected President, the Academy began increasingly to encounter financial difficulties as a result of rising costs. At first it tried to resolve these quietly, but in 1962 the proposed sale of one of its greatest treasures came to the notice of the indignant newspapers. The Academy owned an exceptional work by Leonardo da Vinci, a cartoon, or large preparatory drawing (the word comes from the Italian *cartone*, meaning simply a large piece of paper), of the Virgin and Child with St Anne and St John the Baptist. Little was known about how the cartoon had come to be in the teaching collection of the Schools, and this in part was used to justify its sale (the Michelangelo tondo was reasonably safe, having been bequeathed to the Academy, as we have seen, by Sir George Beaumont). A public

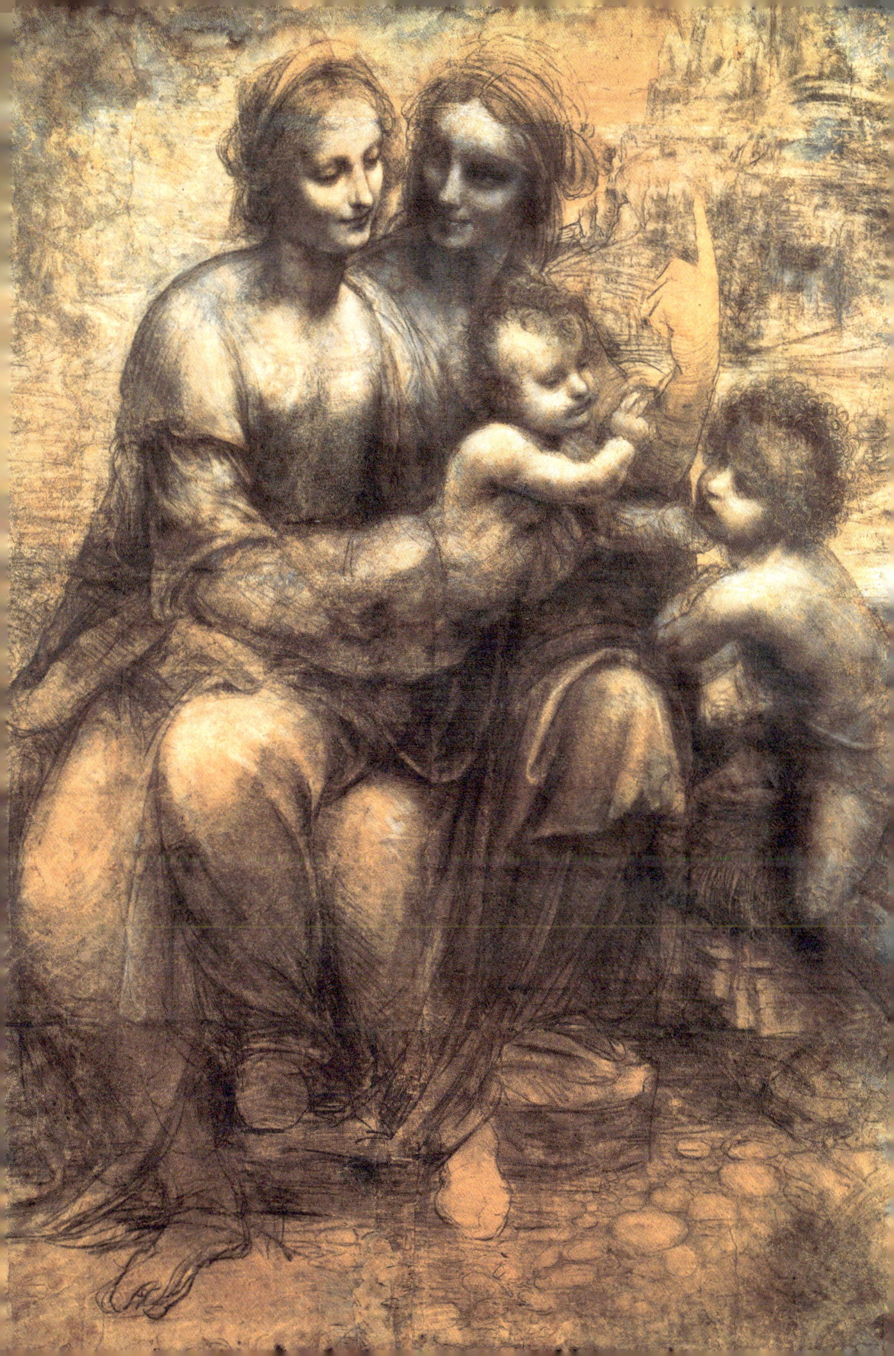

appeal was organised to prevent the cartoon's loss to the nation. The enormous selling price made more headlines and only a little of the opprobrium heaped upon the Academy was mitigated by the National Art Collections Fund's eventual purchase of the work, and its subsequent gift of it to the National Gallery, only a short distance across London.

The more forward-thinking painter Sir Thomas Monnington, PRA from 1966, ensured that in 1967, on the eve of the Academy's bicentenary, female Academicians were invited for the first time to the Annual Dinner, Dame Laura Knight among them. The shades of Angelica Kauffman and Mary Moser must have smiled to themselves ruefully. The following year's Annual Dinner, attended by Her Majesty The Queen and Prince Philip, was the prelude to the Bicentenary Exhibition, which told the story in over 1,000 works of art of the Academy's activities over its two-hundred-year history. The balance sheets remained unsteady, the expense of maintaining Burlington House partly taking the blame.

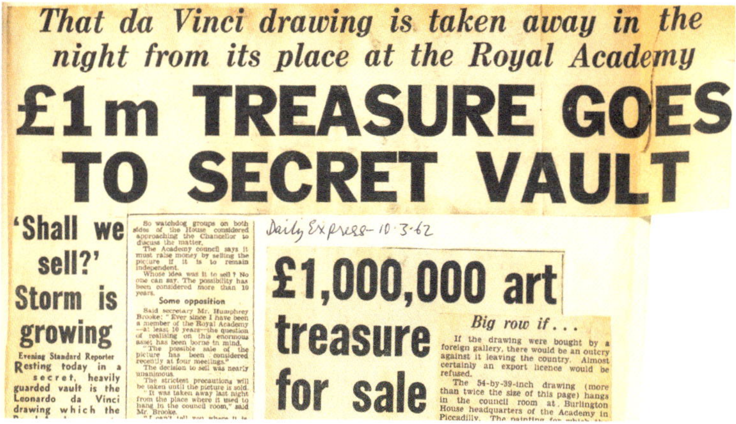

That da Vinci drawing is taken away in the night from its place at the Royal Academy

£1m TREASURE GOES TO SECRET VAULT

'Shall we sell?' Storm is growing

Evening Standard Reporter

Resting today in a secret, heavily guarded vault is the Leonardo da Vinci drawing which the

So watchdog groups on both sides of the House considered approaching the Chancellor to discuss the matter.

The Academy council says it must raise money by selling the picture if it is to remain independent.

Whose idea was it to sell? No one can say. The possibility has been considered more than 10 years.

Some opposition

Said secretary Mr. Humphrey Brooke: "Ever since I have been a member of the Royal Academy—at least 10 years—the question of realising on this enormous asset has been borne in mind.

"The possible sale of the picture has been considered recently at four meetings."

The decision to sell was nearly unanimous.

The strictest precautions will be taken until the picture is sold.

"It was taken away last night from the place where it used to hang in the council room," said Mr. Brooke.

Daily Express 10.3.62

£1,000,000 art treasure for sale

Big row if . . .

If the drawing were bought by a foreign gallery, there would be an outcry against it leaving the country. Almost certainly an export licence would be refused.

The 54-by-39-inch drawing (more than twice the size of this page) hangs in the council room at Burlington House headquarters of the Academy in Piccadilly.

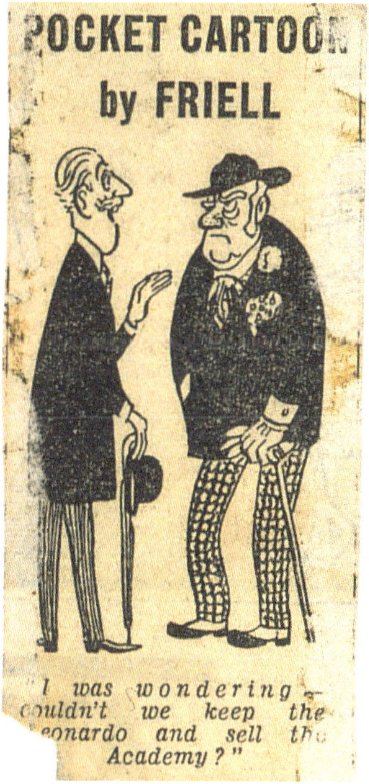

POCKET CARTOON by FRIELL

"I was wondering — couldn't we keep the eonardo and sell th Academy?"

Newspaper cuttings showing the reaction to the Academy's proposed sale of the Leonardo cartoon

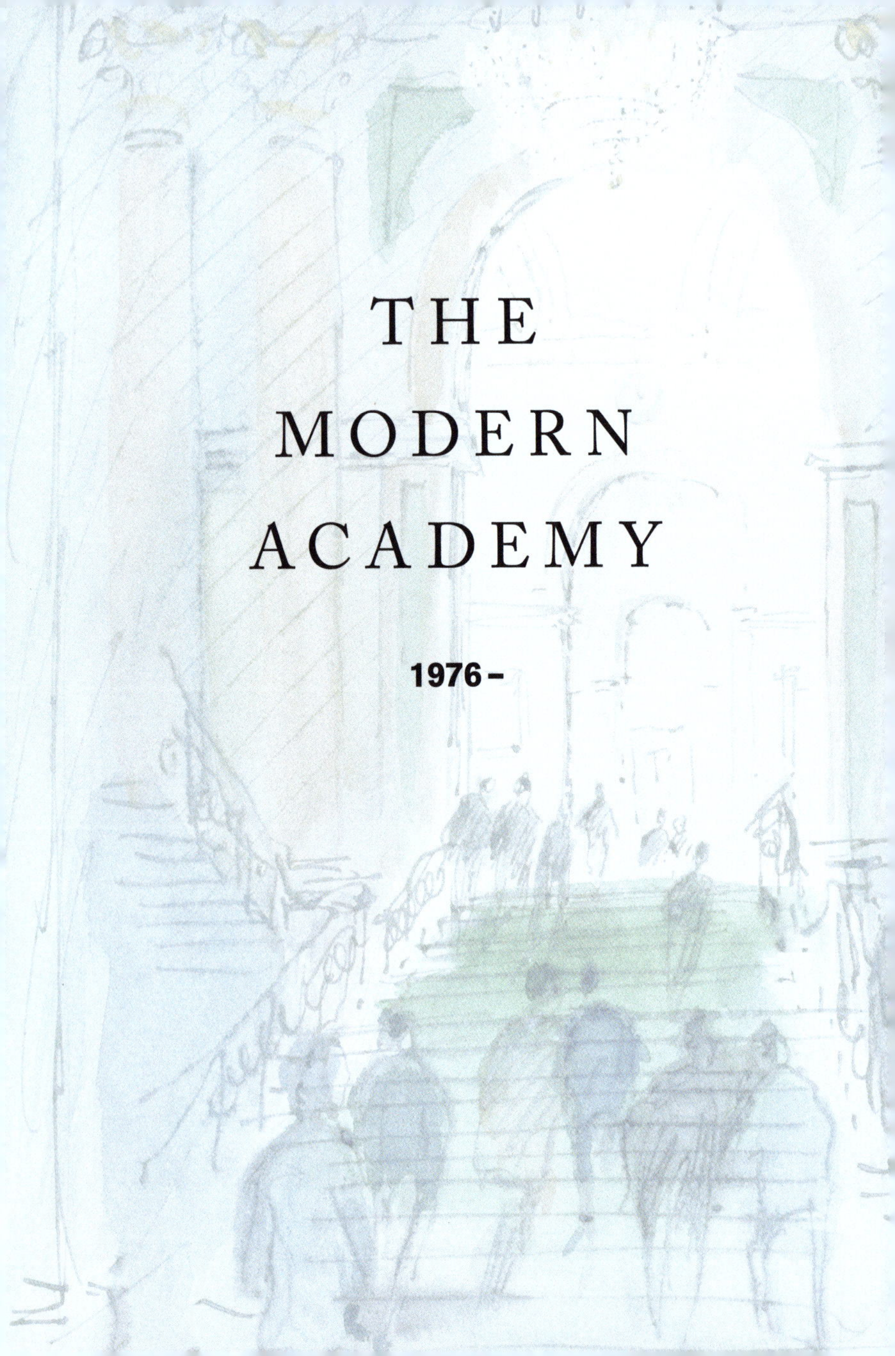

THE MODERN ACADEMY

1976–

The election of the architect Sir Hugh Casson as PRA in 1976 brought renewed vigour and optimism to Burlington House. Casson had worked on the 1951 Festival of Britain, and had a gift for getting the best out of people. He was often to be seen darting to meetings around London in his yellow Mini. Having read a *Spectator* article in which a young curator exhorted the Royal Academy to become 'the major forum for new art again, as it was in its first hundred years', he appointed its author, Norman Rosenthal, as the Royal Academy's Exhibitions Secretary in 1977. This clever move cemented the rise of the international loan exhibition at Burlington House, and coincided with the foundation of the Friends of the Royal Academy, which nowadays numbers over 100,000 members. Rosenthal, a persuasive and passionate curator, was to work for the Academy for thirty years, programming intriguing and critically acclaimed loan exhibitions, among them during Casson's time the influential 'A New Spirit in Painting' (1981).

The painter Sir Roger de Grey succeeded Casson as PRA in 1984, and it was during his presidency that the Jillian and Arthur M. Sackler Wing of Galleries was designed by Norman Foster's practice. Foster ingeniously exploited the unused space between the garden front of Lord Burlington's house and the south wall of Smirke's great galleries by inserting a glass lift and staircase to take visitors up to an airy sculpture landing adjoining the former Diploma Galleries, which he converted into three more intimate spaces, without ornament and ideally suited to a programme of smaller, focused loan exhibitions.

Although revenue was on the increase, thanks to the Academy's rapidly growing Friends scheme and Rosenthal's programme of loan exhibitions, which encompassed at this time a series of synoptic surveys

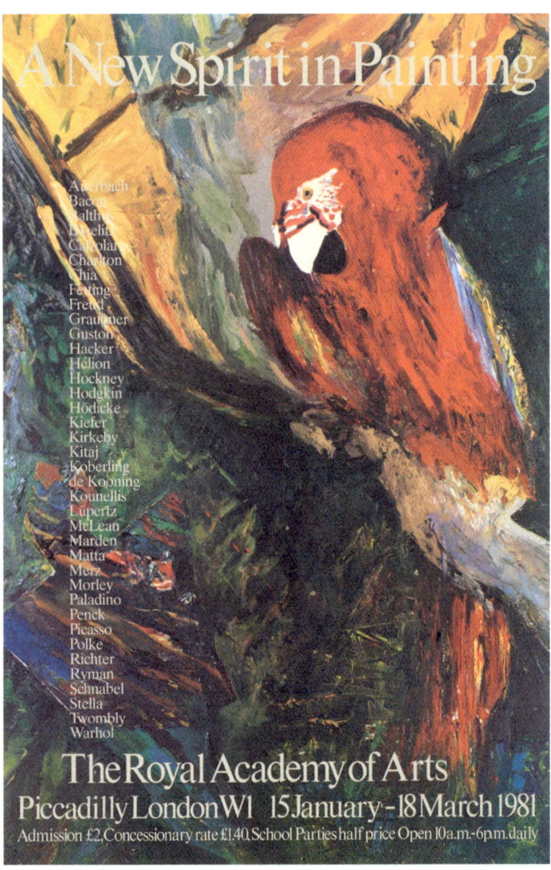

The poster for 'A New Spirit in Painting' (1981)

Foster + Partners designed a glass staircase to take visitors up to the Sackler Wing

Overleaf: Richard Deacon RA's installation of works from the Academy's collections in the Dame Jillian Sackler Sculpture Gallery

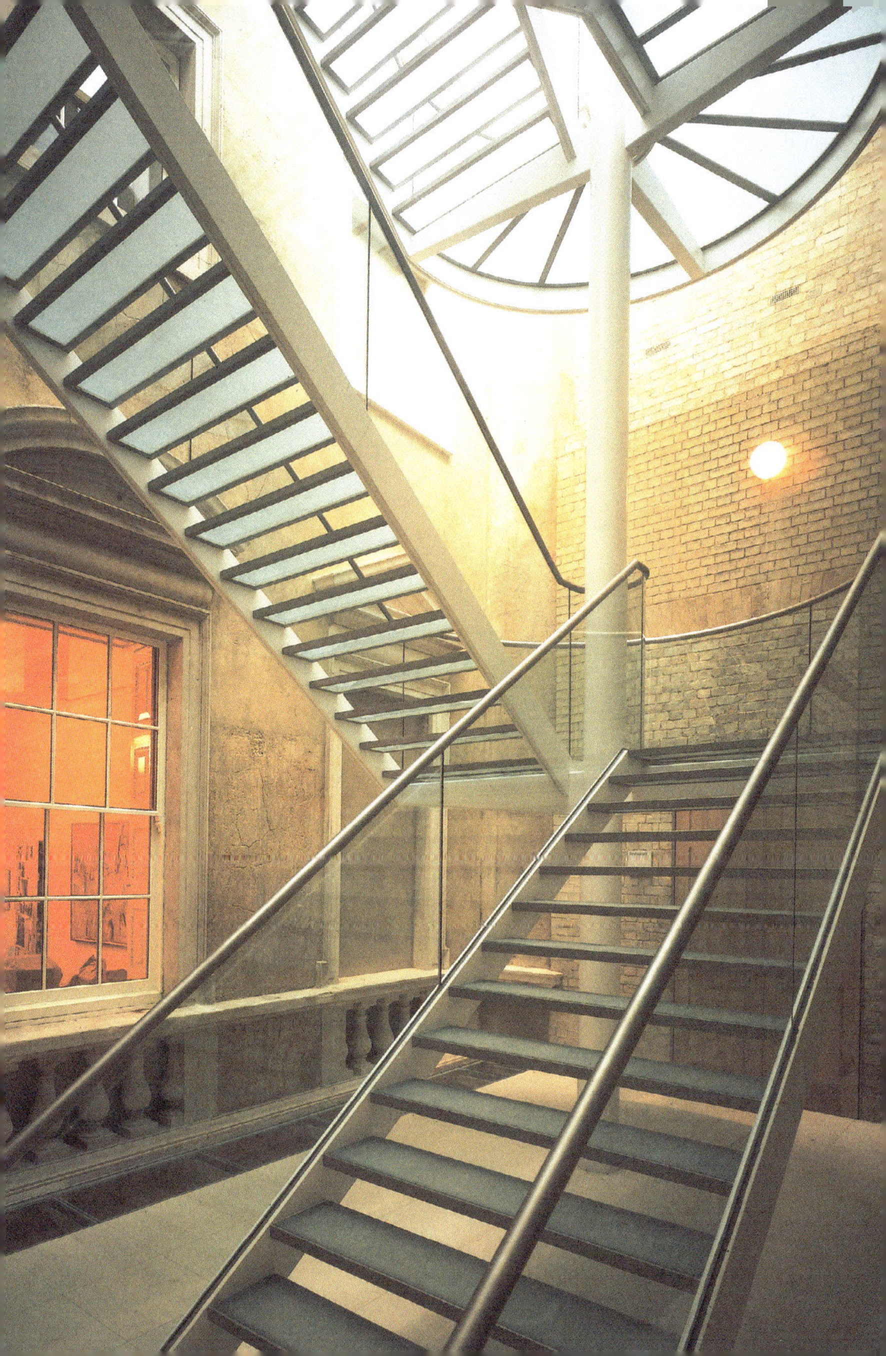

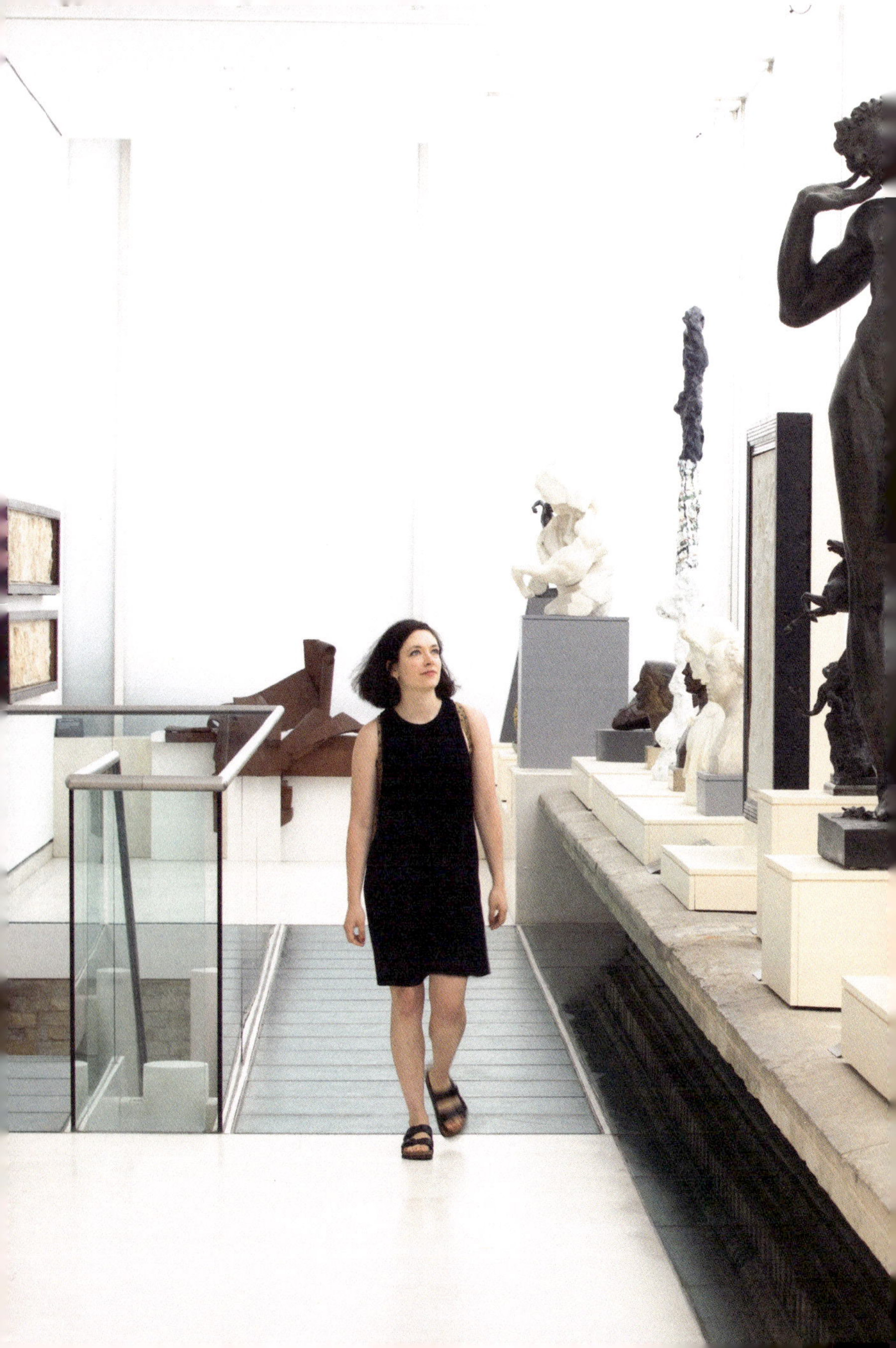

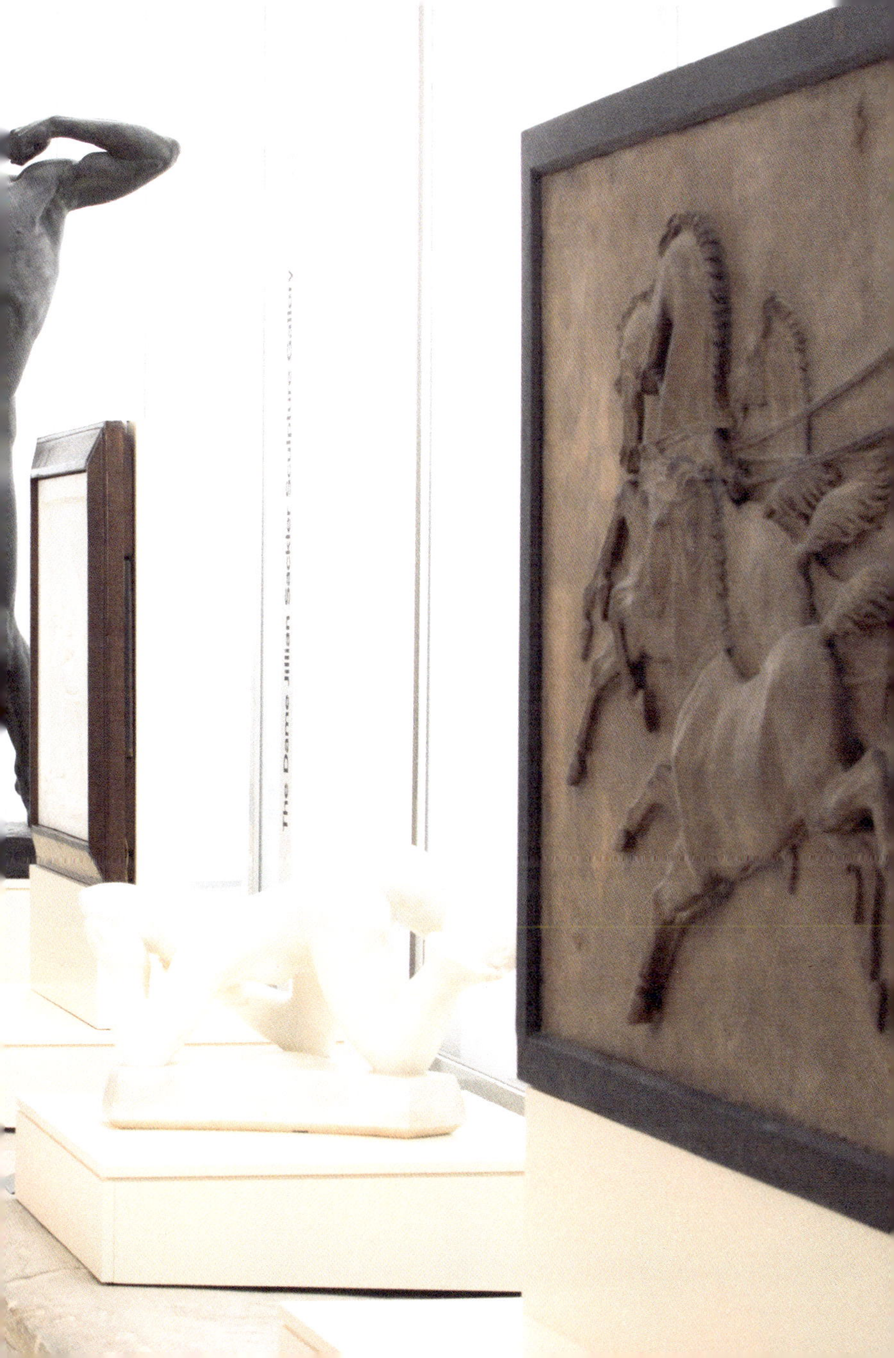
The Dame Jillian Sackler Sculpture Gallery

of twentieth-century art in Germany, Britain, Italy and America, financial stability remained elusive. The presidency of the architect Sir Philip Dowson (1993–99) saw the ambitious exhibition 'Africa: Art of a Continent' (1995) and the controversial 'Sensation' (1997), featuring works from the collection of Charles Saatchi by Damien Hirst, Jake and Dinos Chapman, and Tracey Emin, among other Young British Artists; some have since been elected Royal Academicians. Also on Dowson's watch was the exceptionally popular show 'Monet in the Twentieth Century' (1999), which was seen by some 700,000 visitors.

Dowson was succeeded as PRA in 1999 by the eminent sculptor Phillip King, a student of Anthony Caro and an assistant of Henry Moore. In 2001 the Academy acquired the freehold of 6 Burlington Gardens, whose lease had been given up to the

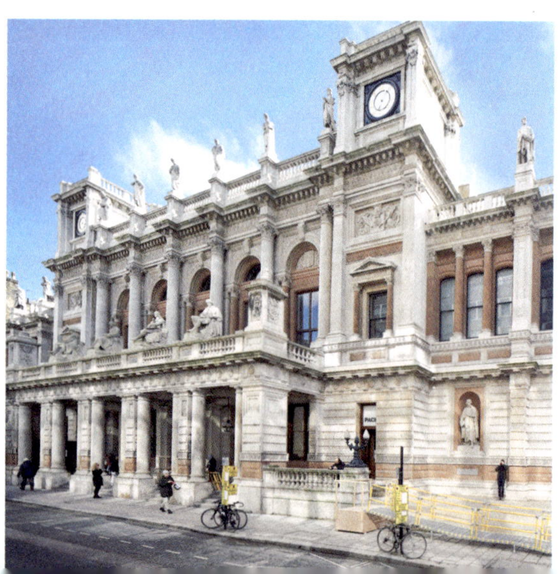

The newly cleaned façade of Burlington Gardens, 2018

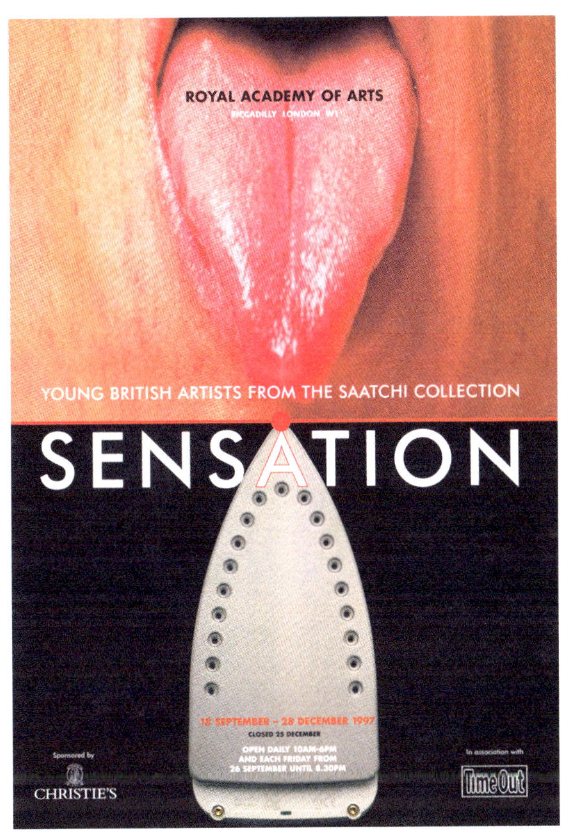

The poster for 'Sensation: Young British Artists from the Saatchi Collection' (1997)

Overleaf: 'David Hockney: A Bigger Picture' (2012) drew more than 600,000 visitors

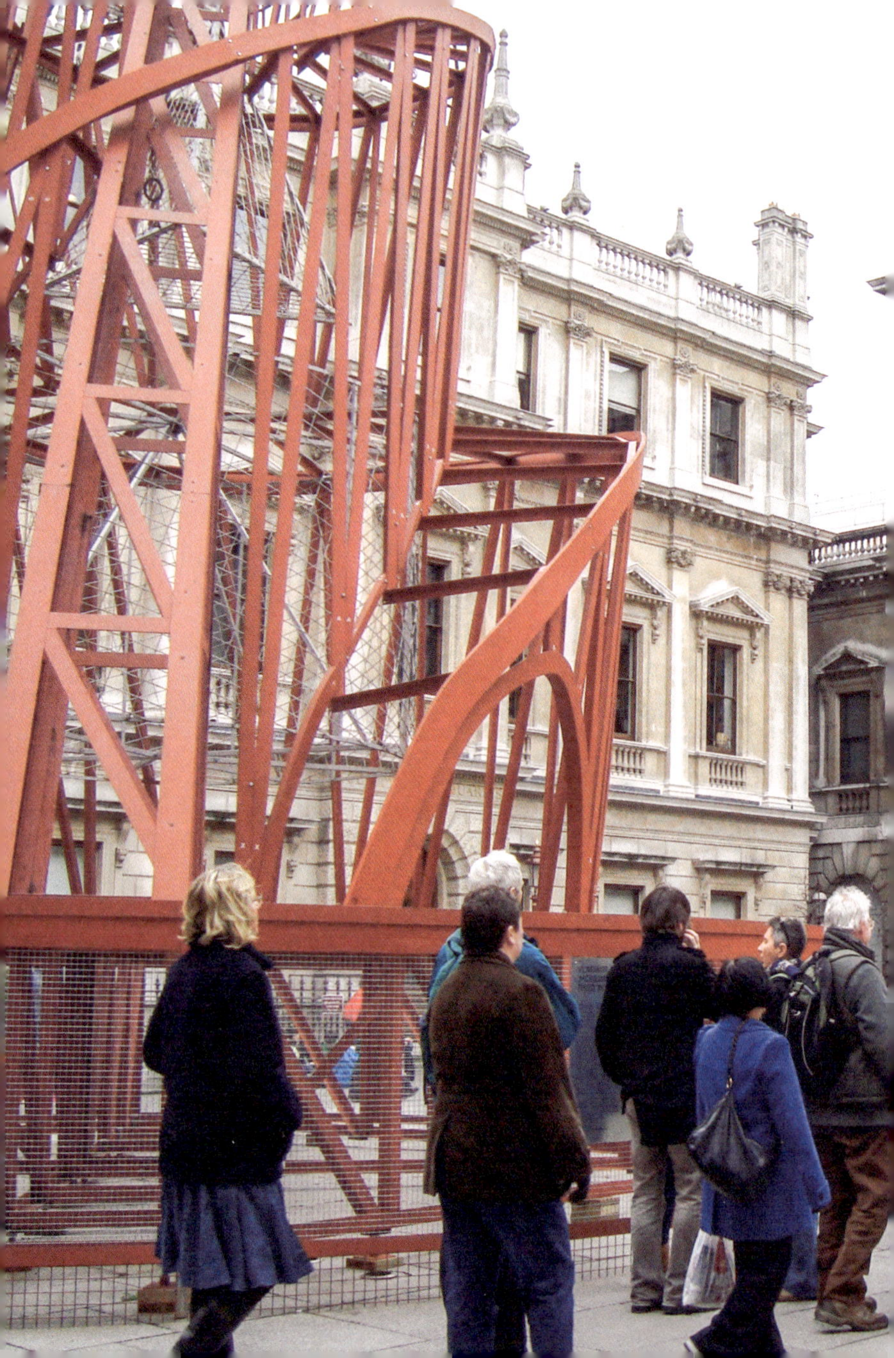

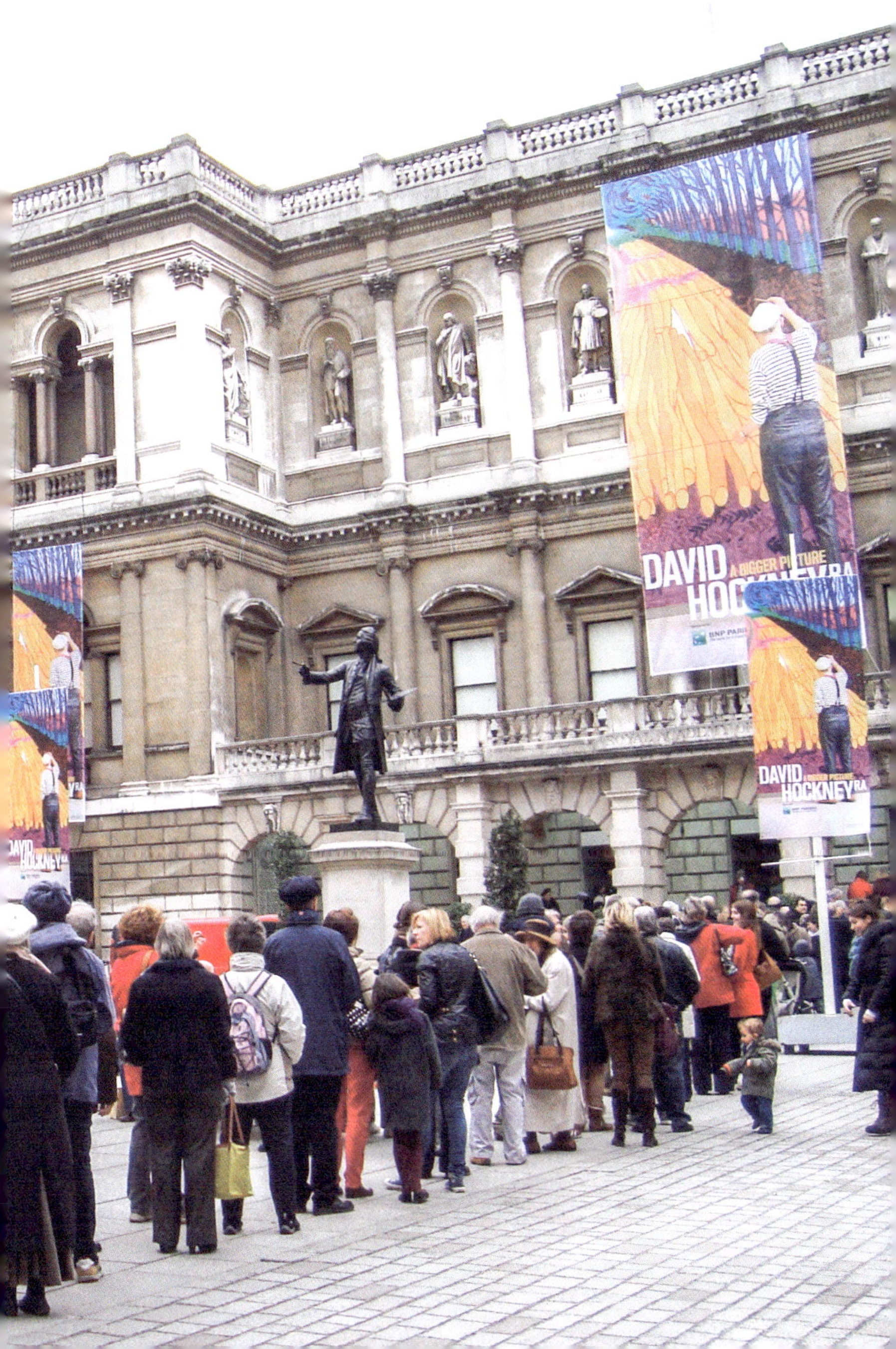
DAVID
A BIGGER PICTURE
DAVID
A BIGGER PICTURE
HOCKNEY RA

Christopher Le Brun PRA wearing the President's medal at the opening reception for 'Charles I: King and Collector' (2018)

The living sculptures Gilbert & George RA were elected in 2017

Overleaf: Michael Craig-Martin RA co-ordinated the Summer Exhibition in 2015

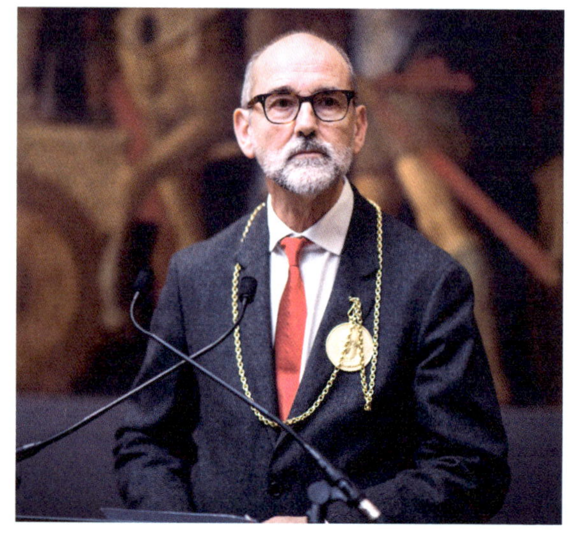

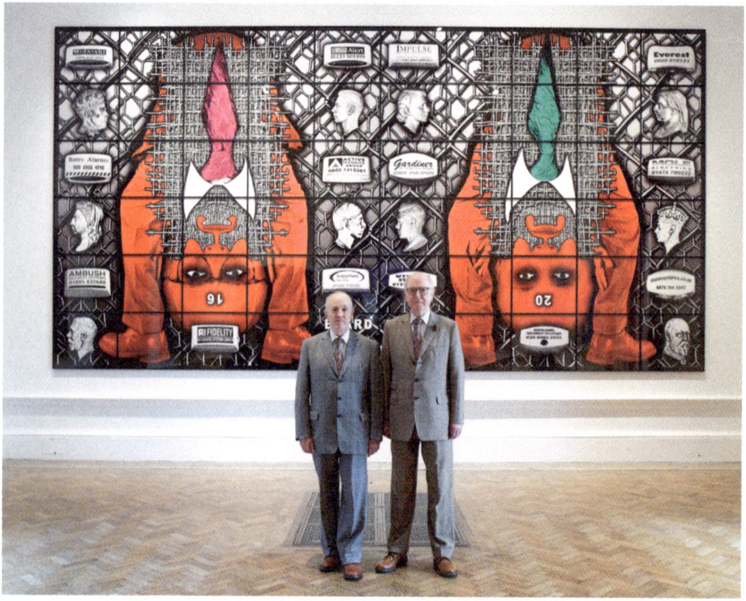

Government by the British Museum when it moved out to consolidate its storage facilities. The grandiose Italianate structure was built between 1867 and 1870 on the part of Burlington House's garden not occupied by Smirke's galleries. Designed as a set of examination halls and laboratories for the University of London by Sir James Pennethorne, 6 Burlington Gardens subsequently came to be occupied by the National Antarctic Expedition and the Civil Service Commission, before its transformation into the Museum of Mankind, which displayed the British Museum's ethnographic collections until 1997.

The Academicians elected the architect Sir Nicholas Grimshaw as their President in 2004. Perhaps best known for his Eurostar terminal at Waterloo Station, Grimshaw instituted further streamlining of the Academy's business practices, and oversaw a number of ambitious and successful loan exhibitions, among them 'China: The Three Emperors' (2005) and 'The Real Van Gogh: The Artist and His Letters' (2010). The painter, sculptor and printmaker Christopher Le Brun took over as PRA in 2011, and has successfully continued the work of planning the unification of Burlington House and Burlington Gardens with Charles Saumarez Smith, Secretary and Chief Executive from 2007. In 2012 one of the Academy's most popular exhibitions ever, 'David Hockney: A Bigger Picture', featured a group of landscapes made near the artist's mother's home in East Yorkshire, and attracted some 600,000 visitors.

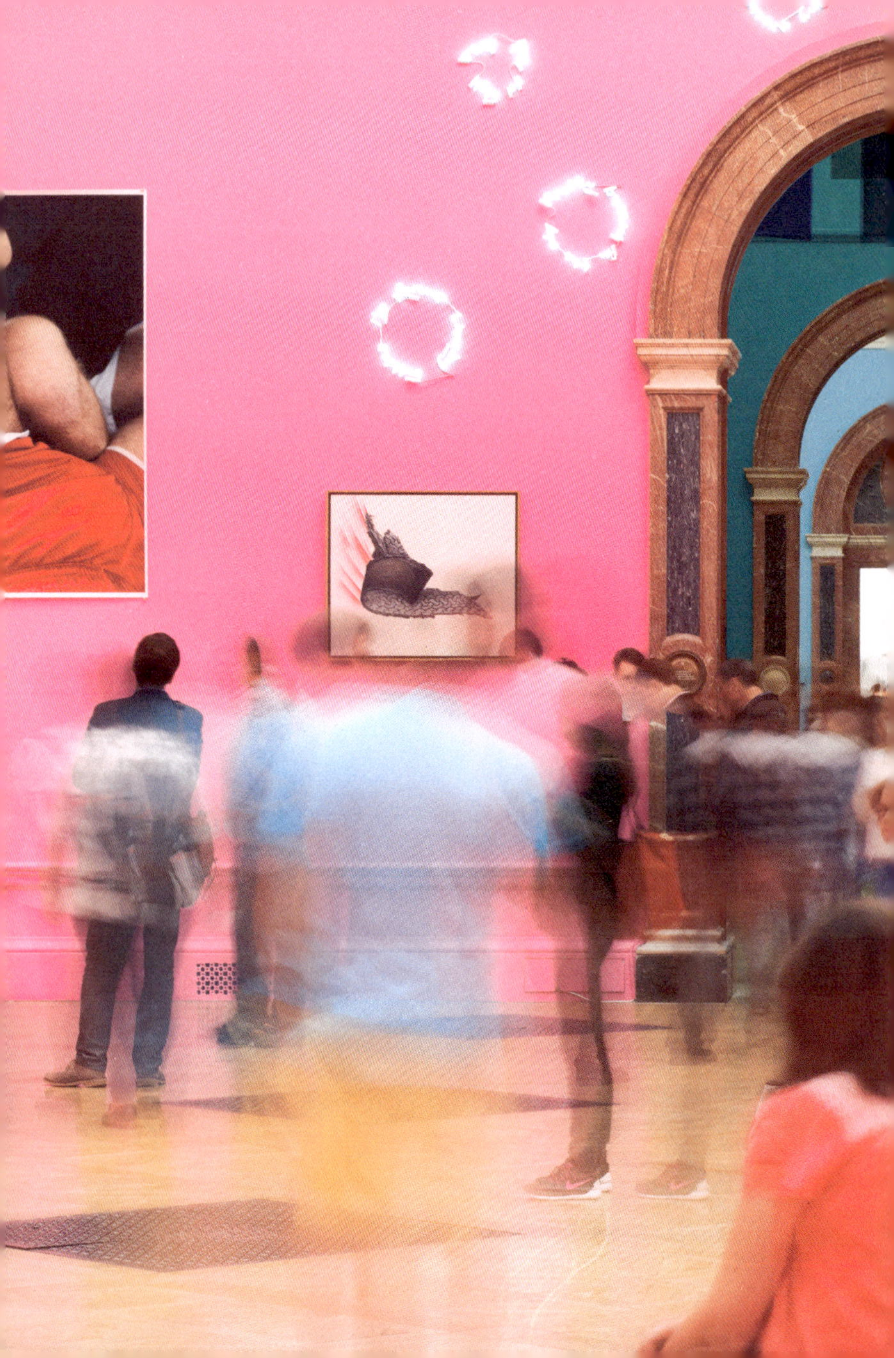

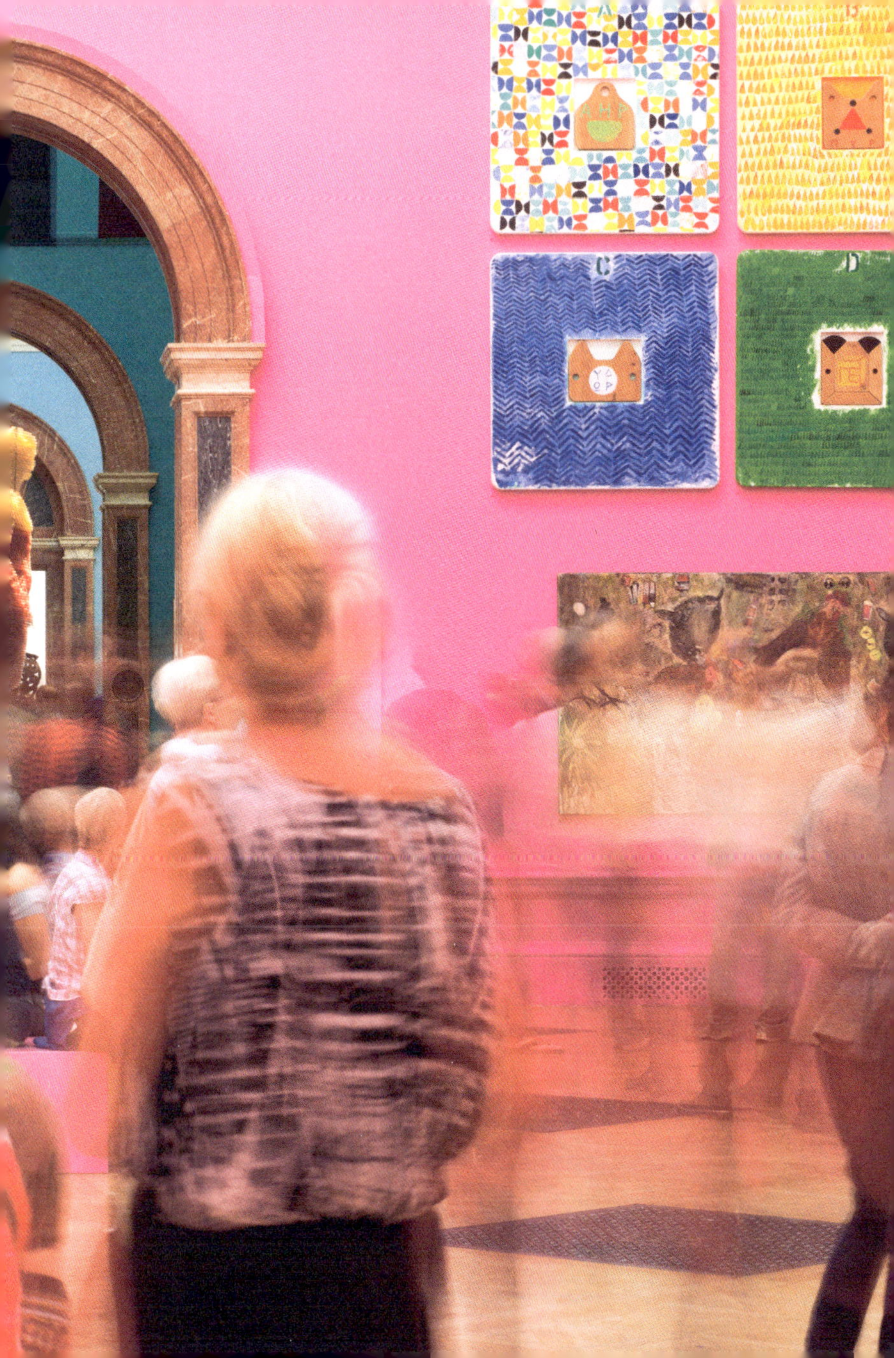

Today's Royal Academicians comprise many more women artists than the two who joined in 1768, and the categories of membership have been broadened to reflect contemporary artistic practice.

The immensely challenging logistical task of unifying a central London estate comprising a Palladian town palace, the capital's finest nineteenth-century exhibition galleries and a substantial Victorian edifice with as yet unrealised potential has occupied many minds, not least those of Sir Michael Hopkins and Sir Colin St John Wilson. Its realisation in 2018, the Royal Academy's 250th anniversary year, at the hands of Sir David Chipperfield, with a new link bridge, galleries and lecture theatre and substantial internal reordering and improvement of the public areas, leaves the Academy in the strongest position it has yet enjoyed to promote 'the Arts of Design' for another quarter of a millennium.

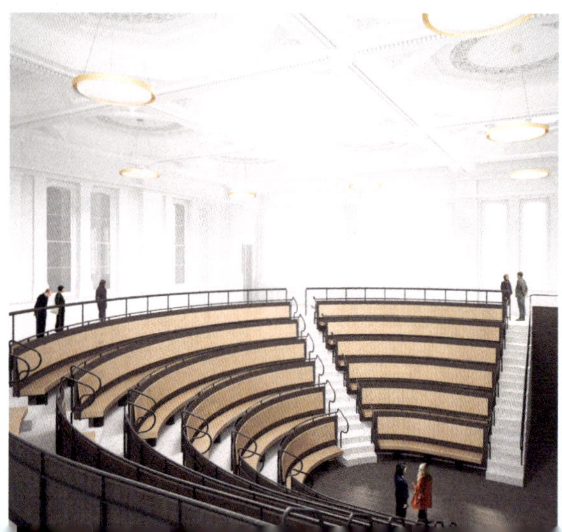

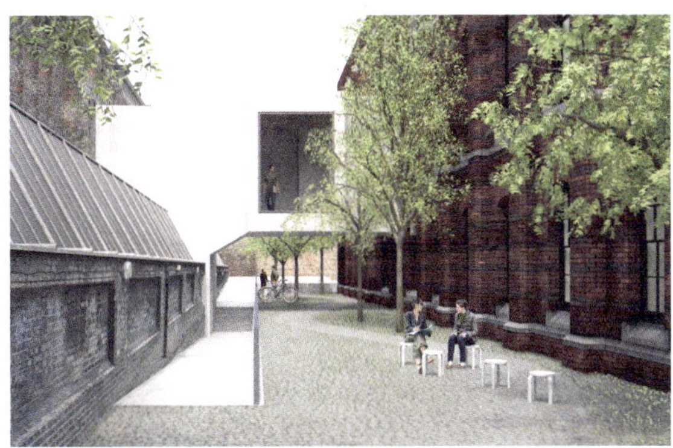

Left: the Benjamin West Lecture Theatre at Burlington Gardens

The Weston Bridge, linking Burlington House and Burlington Gardens

Construction of the Weston Bridge, 2018

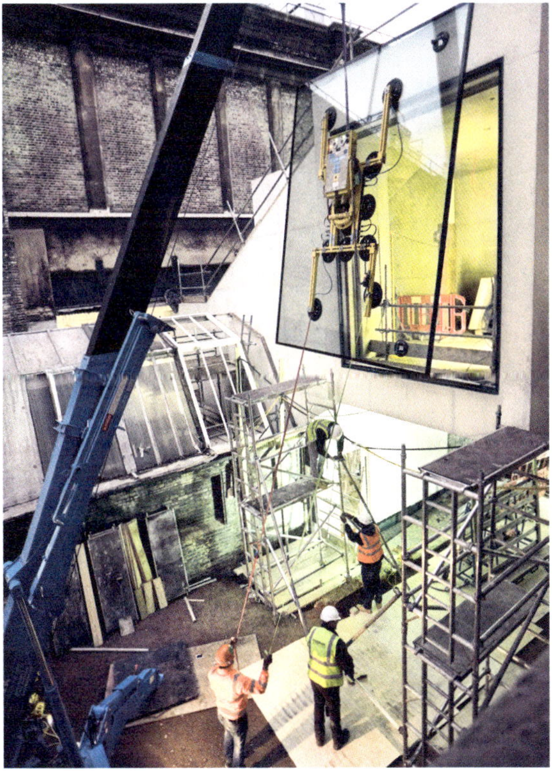

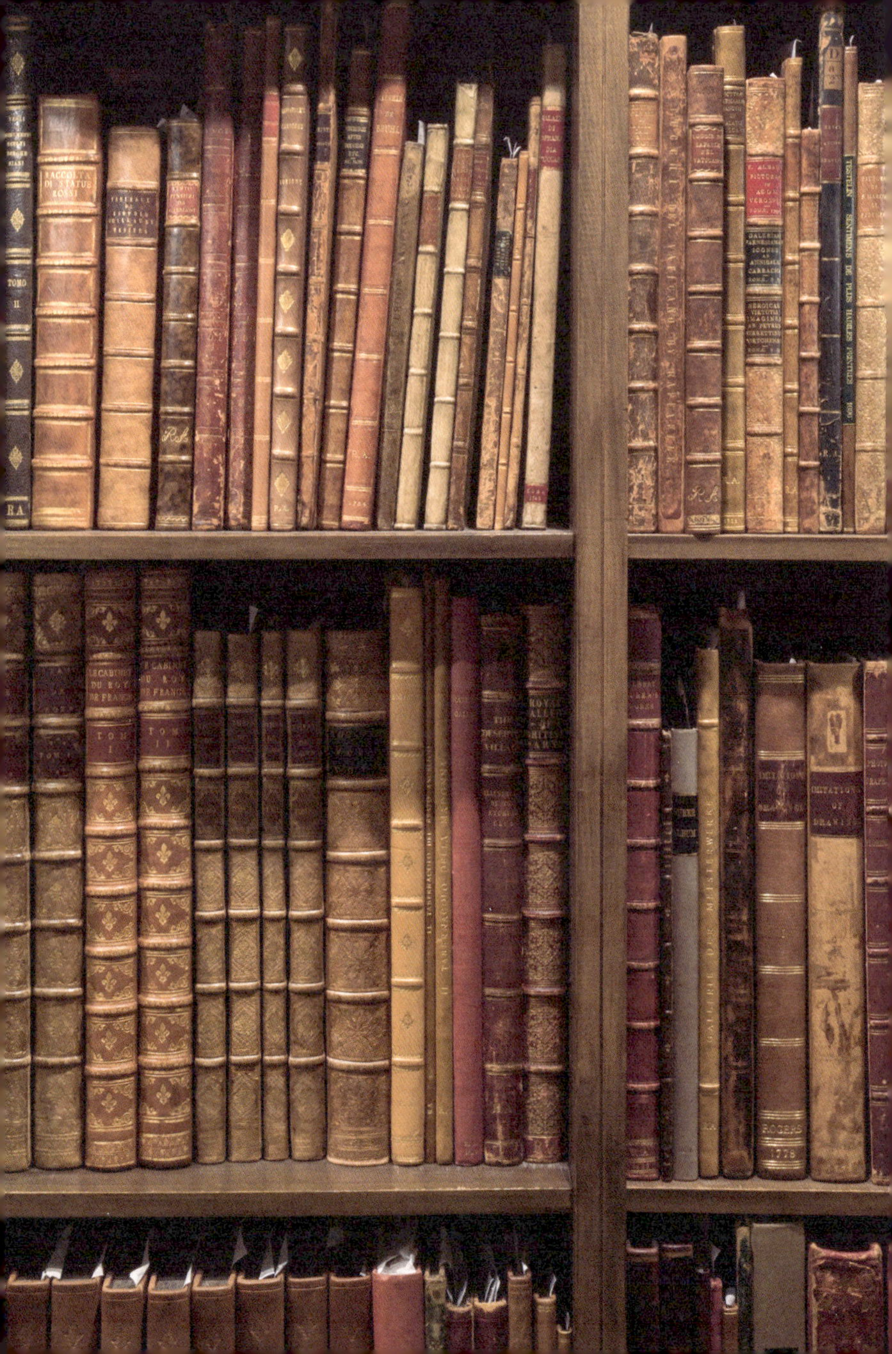

RACCOLTA DI STATUE
TOMO II.
R.A.
LE CABINET DU ROY DE FRANCE
TOM I
TOM II
IMITATIONS OF DRAWINGS
ROGERS
1778

Alison Cole, *Michelangelo: The Taddei Tondo*, London, 2017

James Fenton, *School of Genius: A History of the Royal Academy of Arts*, London, 2006

Mark Hallett and Sarah Victoria Turner, with Jessica Feather, *The Great Spectacle: 250 Years of the Royal Academy Summer Exhibition*, exh. cat., Royal Academy of Arts, London, 2018

Holger Hoock, *The King's Artists: The Royal Academy of Arts and the Politics of British Culture, 1760–1840*, Oxford, 2003

Richard Humphreys, *John Constable: The Leaping Horse*, London, 2018

Sidney C. Hutchison, *The History of the Royal Academy, 1768–1986*, London, 1986

Sidney C. Hutchison, *The Homes of the Royal Academy*, London, 1956

Sir Walter R. M. Lamb, *The Royal Academy: A Short History of Its Foundation and Development*, London, 1951

William Sandby, *The History of the Royal Academy of Arts from Its Foundation in 1768 to the Present Time, with Biographical Notices of All the Members*, 2 vols, London, 1862

Charles Saumarez Smith, *The Company of Artists: The Origins of the Royal Academy of Arts in London*, London, 2012

Nicholas Savage, *Burlington House: Home of the Royal Academy of Arts*, London, 2018

Robin Simon (ed.), *The Royal Academy of Arts: History and Collections*, New Haven and London, 2018

David H. Solkin, *Art on the Line: The Royal Academy Exhibitions at Somerset House, 1780–1836*, exh. cat., Courtauld Institute of Art, London, 2001

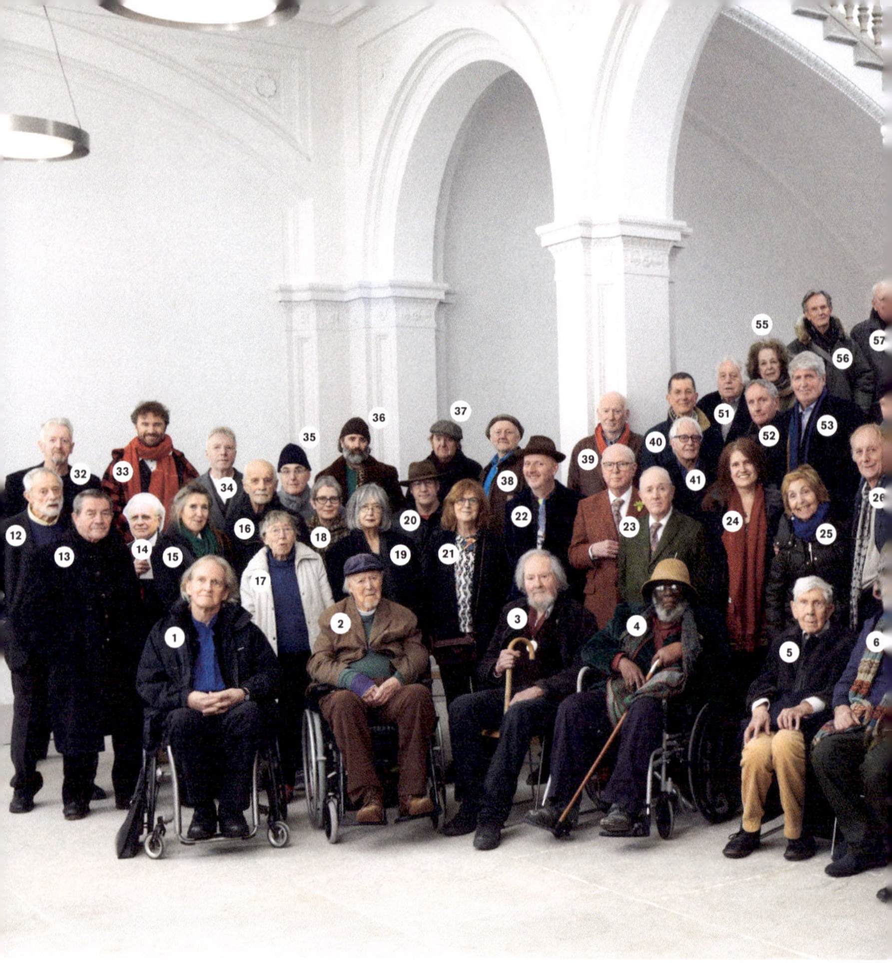

Pictured
1. Alan Stanton
2. Jeffery Camp
3. Anthony Eyton
4. Frank Bowling
5. Trevor Dannatt
6. Tom Phillips
7. Anthony Whishaw
8. Yinka Shonibare
9. Diana Armfield
10. Paul Koralek
11. Edward Cullinan
12. Peter Freeth
13. Gus Cummins
14. Ian Ritchie
15. Vanessa Jackson
16. Phillip King
17. Olwyn Bowey
18. Lisa Milroy
19. Rose Wylie
20. Tim Shaw
21. Mali Morris
22. Bob & Roberta Smith
23. Gilbert & George
24. Anne Desmet
25. Paula Rego
26. Norman Ackroyd
27. Christopher Le Brun
28. Norman Foster
29. Alison Wilding
30. Farshid Moussavi
31. Phyllida Barlow
32. David Mach
33. Thomas Heatherwick
34. Hughie O'Donoghue
35. Humphrey Ocean
36. Mike Nelson
37. Richard Wilson
38. Stephen Chambers
39. Bill Woodrow
40. Antony Gormley
41. Terry Setch
42. Grayson Perry
43. Cathie Pilkington
44. Timothy Hyman
45. Brian Catling
46. Nicholas Grimshaw
47. Paul Huxley

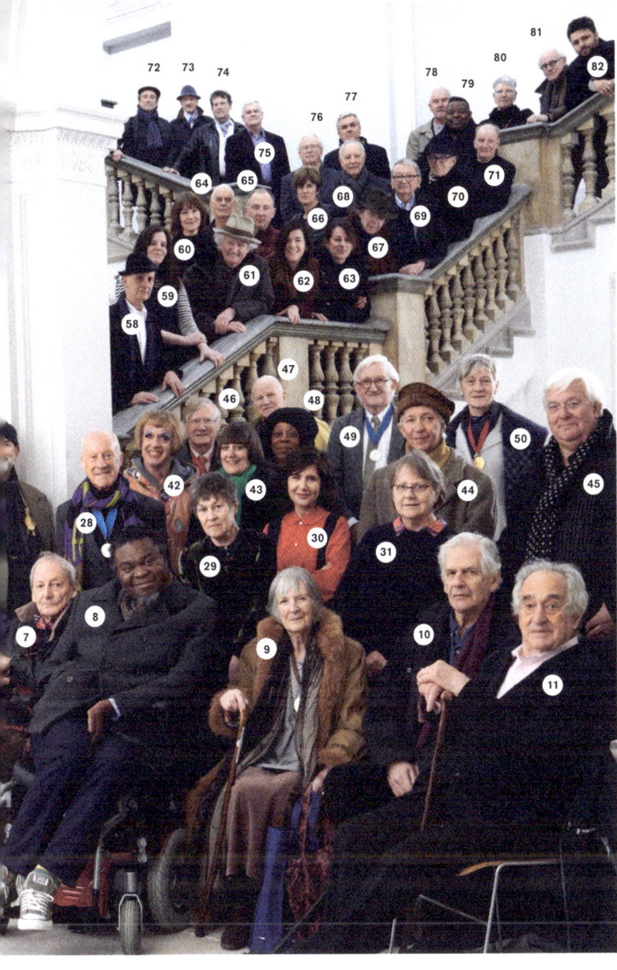

48. Sonia Boyce
49. Spencer de Grey
50. Rebecca Salter
51. Michael Sandle
52. Chris Orr
53. John Maine
54. James Butler
55. Tess Jaray
56. Nigel Hall
57. Basil Beattie
58. David Remfry
59. Chantal Joffe

60. Fiona Rae
61. Ken Howard
62. Fiona Banner
63. Rebecca Warren
64. Richard Long
65. Gary Hume
66. Emma Stibbon
67. Will Alsop
68. Chris Wilkinson
69. Michael Hopkins
70. Peter Cook
71. Jock McFadyen

72. Peter Randall-Page
73. Allen Jones
74. Eric Parry
75. Stephen Cox
76. Ian McKeever
77. Neil Jeffries
78. Tony Bevan
79. Isaac Julien
80. Ann Christopher
81. John Carter
82. Conrad Shawcross

Not pictured
David Adjaye
Ron Arad
Gordon Benson
Elizabeth Blackadder
David Chipperfield
Eileen Cooper
Tony Cragg
Michael Craig-Martin
Fred Cuming
Richard Deacon
Tacita Dean
Jennifer Dickson
Kenneth Draper
Jennifer Durrant
Tracey Emin
Stephen Farthing
Piers Gough
Anthony Green
David Hockney
Louisa Hutton
Bill Jacklin
Eva Jiricna
Anish Kapoor
Bryan Kneale
Michael Landy
Sonia Lawson
Leonard McComb
Dhruva Mistry
Mick Moon
David Nash
Cornelia Parker
Barbara Rae
Richard Rogers
Mick Rooney
Eva Rothschild
Jenny Saville
Sean Scully
Philip Sutton
Wolfgang Tillmans
Joe Tilson
David Tindle
William Tucker
Gillian Wearing
Jane and Louise Wilson
John Wragg

General Assembly of the Royal Academicians, 19 March 2018. Photograph by Johnnie Shand Kydd

2–3 Lee Krasner, *The Eye Is the First Circle*, 1960, in the exhibition 'Abstract Expressionism' (2016) at the Royal Academy. © ARS, NY and DACS, London, 2018. Photo © James Harris

4 Jim Lambie, 'Zobop' staircase installation for the 247th Summer Exhibition (2015) at the Royal Academy. © Jim Lambie, courtesy Sadie Coles HQ, London

6 The façade of Burlington House, with Alfred Drury RA's bronze statue of Sir Joshua Reynolds

9 The Library of the Royal Academy, Burlington House

10–11 An iPad drawing course in the Life Room as part of the Academic Programme, 2017, led by Mark Hampson, Head of Fine Art Processes for the RA Schools. The model is Dominic Blake. Photo Evan Hutchinson

12 A children's learning workshop at the Royal Academy, 2017. Photo © Roy Matthews

14–15 General Assembly of the Royal Academicians in the entrance hall, Burlington Gardens, 19 March 2018. Photo Johnnie Shand Kydd

16 125 Pall Mall, the Royal Academy's first home. Wood engraving, 12.3 x 9 cm. British Museum, London. © The Trustees of the British Museum

18 Sir Joshua Reynolds PRA (1723–1792), *King George III*, 1779. Oil on canvas, 227.4 x 185.5 cm. © Royal Academy of Arts, London. Photo John Hammond

19 Sir Joshua Reynolds PRA (1723–1792), *Sir William Chambers*, *c.* 1780. Oil on panel, 129 x 103.2 cm. © Royal Academy of Arts, London. Photo Prudence Cuming Associates Ltd

20a Sir Joshua Reynolds PRA (1723–1792), *Self-portrait*, *c.* 1780. Oil on panel, 127 x 101.6 cm. © Royal Academy of Arts, London. Photo John Hammond

20b Detail of the Royal Academy's Instrument of Foundation, signed by King George III on 10 December 1768: 'I approve of this Plan, let it be put into execution.' © Royal Academy of Arts, London

22–23 Johann Zoffany RA (1733–1810), *The Academicians of the Royal Academy*, 1771–72. Oil on canvas, 100.7 x 147.3 cm. Royal Collection. © Her Majesty Queen Elizabeth II

24 Thomas Malton (1748–1804), *St Mary's Church and Somerset House in the Strand*, 5 November 1796 (detail). Etching and aquatint, 30.5 x 21.3 cm. © Royal Academy of Arts, London

26 Henry Singleton (1766–1839), *The Royal Academicians in General Assembly*, 1795. Oil on canvas, 198.1 x 259 cm. © Royal Academy of Arts, London. Photo Prudence Cuming Associates Ltd

27 Thomas Rowlandson (1756–1827), *The Exhibition 'Stare-Case', Somerset House*, *c.* 1800. Watercolour with grey and brown wash on paper, 44.7 x 29.8 cm. Yale Center for British Art, New Haven. Paul Mellon Collection

28 Pietro Antonio Martini (1738–1797), after Johann Heinrich Ramberg (1763–1840), *The Exhibition of the Royal Academy*, 1787. Line engraving, 32 x 49.1 cm. © Royal Academy of Arts, London. Photo Prudence Cuming Associates Ltd

30a Thomas Gainsborough RA (1727–1788), *Romantic Landscape with Sheep at a Spring*, *c.* 1783. Oil on canvas, 153.7 x 186.7 cm. © Royal Academy of Arts, London. Photo Prudence Cuming Associates Ltd

30b J. M. W. Turner RA (1775–1851), *Dolbadern Castle*, 1800. Oil on canvas,

119.4 x 90.2 cm. © Royal Academy of Arts, London. Photo Prudence Cuming Associates Ltd

31 John Constable RA (1776–1837), *A Boat Passing a Lock*, 1826. Oil on canvas, 101.6 x 127 cm. © Royal Academy of Arts, London. Photo Prudence Cuming Associates Ltd

32–33 John Constable RA (1776–1837), *The Leaping Horse*, 1825. Oil on canvas, 142 x 187.3 cm. © Royal Academy of Arts, London. Photo Prudence Cuming Associates Ltd

34–35 A still from Mike Leigh's film *Mr Turner* (2014), showing Timothy Spall in the title role, retouching a work on one of the Varnishing Days at the Annual Exhibition. © Thin Man Films Ltd. Photo Simon Mein

36a Benjamin West PRA (1738–1820), *Self-portrait*, 1793. Oil on panel, 101.5 x 132 cm. © Royal Academy of Arts, London. Photo John Hammond

36b Sir Thomas Lawrence PRA (1769–1830), *Self-portrait*, *c.* 1825. Oil on canvas, 91 x 71.4 cm. © Royal Academy of Arts, London

38–39 Giampietrino (fl *c.* 1500–1550), after Leonardo da Vinci (1452–1519), *The Last Supper*, *c.* 1520. Previously attributed to Marco D'Oggiono (*c.* 1470–*c.* 1549). Oil on canvas, 302 x 785 cm. © Royal Academy of Arts, London. Photo Prudence Cuming Associates Ltd

39 Michelangelo Buonarroti (1475–1564), *The Virgin and Child with the Infant St John*, the Taddei Tondo, *c.* 1504–05. Marble relief, diameter 106.8 cm. © Royal Academy of Arts, London

40 Attributed to Edmund Evans (1826–1905), *The Royal Academy, Trafalgar Square*, 1862 (detail). Wood engraving, 18.6 x 10.8 cm. Frontispiece of William Sandby (1717 1799), *The History of the Royal Academy of Arts…*, London, 1862, vol. 1. © Royal Academy of Arts, London. Photo Andy Johnson

42–43 Mason Jackson (1819–1903), *Taking in the Pictures at the RA*, April 1866. Engraved illustration. Photo Mansell / The LIFE Picture Collection / Getty Images

43 William Payne (1760–1830), *Private View of the Royal Academy*, 1858. Watercolour and graphite with pen and black ink on paper, 9.5 x 10.5 cm. Yale Center for British Art, New Haven

44–45 William Wilkins RA (1778–1839), *The Galleries and Ground Floor of the National Gallery, Trafalgar Square*, 1836: 'N.B. – The part coloured Red is appropriated to the Royal Academy.' Engraved illustration, published 16 August 1836. © The National Gallery, London

46a Sir John Everett Millais Bt PRA (1829–1896), *Ophelia*, 1851–52. Oil on canvas, 76.2 x 111.8 cm. Tate Britain, London. Presented by Sir Henry Tate, 1894. N01506 © Tate, London, 2018

46b Sir John Everett Millais Bt PRA (1829–1896), *John Ruskin*, 1853–54. Oil on canvas, 78.7 x 68 cm. © Ashmolean Museum, University of Oxford

48 Sydney Smirke RA (1798–1877), *Burlington House, Piccadilly: Elevation Showing Proposed Alteration of the South Front*, March 1867 (detail). Pencil and wash, 39 x 45.5 cm. © Royal Academy of Arts, London

51a Sir Francis Grant PRA (1803–1878), *Self-portrait*, 1876. Oil on canvas, 75 x 64 cm. © Royal Academy of Arts, London. Photo John Hammond

51b Johannes Kip (1652/53–1722), after Leonard Knyff (1650–1722), *Burlington*

House in Pickadilly, from *Britannia Illustrata*, London, 1707, plate 29 (detail). Etching, 32.5 x 47.8 cm. © Royal Academy of Arts, London

52a William Aikman (1682–1731), *William Kent*, *c.* 1723–25. Oil on canvas, 197 x 104 cm. © National Portrait Gallery, London

52b Elevated view of Burlington House, Piccadilly, 1866. Wood engraving from the *Illustrated London News*, 15 September 1866

53 The Saloon, Burlington House, looking east through the enfilade. Photo © Richard Bryant

55a Stephen Ayling (fl. 1860–1872), *The South Front of Burlington House*, *c.* 1860s. Monotone photograph, 19 x 27.4 cm. © Royal Academy of Arts, London

55b Stephen Ayling (fl. 1860–1872), *Burlington House, Piccadilly: East Offices, Colonnade and Gateway*, *c.* 1860s. Albumen print mounted on card, 26.9 x 15.6 cm. © Royal Academy of Arts, London. Photo Prudence Cuming Associates Ltd

56–57 Sydney Smirke RA (1798–1877), *Design for Gallery III, Burlington House, Piccadilly*, *c.* 1866–67. Pencil and pen with black ink, coloured washes and gouache, 32.5 x 29 cm. © Royal Academy of Arts, London. Photo Prudence Cuming Associates Ltd

59 Charles West Cope RA (1811–1890), *The Council of the Royal Academy Selecting Pictures for the Exhibition, 1875*, 1876. Oil on canvas, 145.2 x 220.1 cm. © Royal Academy of Arts, London. Photo John Hammond

60 George Frederic Watts RA (1817–1904), *Frederic, Lord Leighton PRA*, 1888. Oil on canvas, 115 x 88 cm. © Royal Academy of Arts, London. Photo John Hammond

62–63 After Charles Paul Renouard (1845–1924), *The Royal Academy*. Wood engravings from *The Graphic*, 7 May 1887. © Royal Academy of Arts, London

64 William Powell Frith RA (1819–1909), *A Private View at the Royal Academy, 1881*, 1883. Oil on canvas, 102 x 195 cm. Private collection. Photo © a Pope Family Trust / Martin Beisly

65 Sir Hamo Thornycroft RA (1850–1925), *Teucer*, 1881. Bronze, height 44 cm. © Royal Academy of Arts, London. Given by Elfrida Manning, 1987

66 Gallery IX, Burlington House, after the explosion of a German bomb on 24 September 1917 (detail). Photograph, 23.8 x 28.8 cm. © Royal Academy of Arts, London

68 London and North Eastern Railway poster for the 'Exhibition of Italian Art' (1930) at the Royal Academy

69 Walter Sickert RA (1860–1942), *Santa Maria della Salute, Venice*, *c.* 1901. Oil on canvas, 56 x 46 cm. © Royal Academy of Arts, London. Photo John Hammond

70l Wyndham Lewis (1882–1957), *T. S. Eliot*, 1938. Oil on canvas, 133.3 x 85.5 cm. Durban Municipal Art Gallery. © The Wyndham Lewis Memorial Trust / Bridgeman Images

70r Robert Lutyens (1901–1972), *Sir Edwin Lutyens*, 1959. Oil on canvas, 25.4 x 22.9 cm. © National Portrait Gallery, London

71 Unknown photographer, *Alfred Munnings PRA with Christmas Greetings*, 1957–58. © Estate of Sir Alfred Munnings, Dedham, Essex. All rights reserved, DACS 2018

73 Leonardo da Vinci (1452–1519), *The Virgin and Child with St Anne and St John the Baptist*, the Burlington House Cartoon, *c.* 1499–1500. Charcoal (and possibly wash) heightened with white chalk on paper, mounted on canvas, 141.5 x 104.6 cm. © The National Gallery, London. Purchased with a special grant and contributions from The Art Fund, The Pilgrim Trust, and through a public appeal organised by The Art Fund, 1962

75 Newspaper cuttings showing the reaction to the Academy's proposed sale of the Leonardo cartoon

76 Sir Hugh Casson PRA (1910–1999), *The Great Staircase, Burlington House*, 1977 (detail). Watercolour with pen and ink on paper, 34.7 x 25 cm. Copyright © Hugh Casson PRA. Photo © Royal Academy of Arts, London. Photo Prudence Cuming Associates Ltd

78 The poster for the exhibition 'A New Spirit in Painting' (1981). The poster shows a detail from Malcolm Morley (b. 1931), *Parrots*, 1979. Oil on canvas, 119.5 x 148.5 cm. Collection Robert Miller, New York. © Malcolm Morley

79 The glass staircase that leads up to the Sackler Wing of Galleries, Burlington House, designed by Foster + Partners. Photo Dennis Gilbert / VIEW

80–81 The Dame Jillian Sackler Sculpture Gallery outside the Sackler Wing of Galleries, Burlington House, showing the arrangement of sculpture curated by Richard Deacon RA in 2017. Photo © David Parry Photography

82 The newly cleaned façade of the Royal Academy's Burlington Gardens building, March 2018. Photo Rory Mulvey

83 The poster for the exhibition 'Sensation: Young British Artists from the Saatchi Collection' (1997). © Royal Academy of Arts, London

84–85 Queues for the exhibition 'David Hockney: A Bigger Picture' (2012) in the Annenberg Courtyard. © Royal Academy of Arts, London

86a Christopher Le Brun PRA speaking at the opening reception of the exhibition 'Charles I: King and Collector', 23 January 2018. Photo Thomas Alexander Photography

86b Gilbert & George RA at the 248th Summer Exhibition (2016). Photo Stephen White

88–89 The 247th Summer Exhibition (2015), co-ordinated by Michael Craig-Martin RA. Photo © James Harris. Right: Joe Tilson RA (b. 1928), *The Four Elements, A–D*, 2013. Mixed media, each 120 x 120 cm. © Joe Tilson, courtesy Marlborough Fine Art

90 The Benjamin West Lecture Theatre at Burlington Gardens, designed by Sir David Chipperfield RA. © David Chipperfield Architects

91a Sir David Chipperfield's Weston Bridge connects Burlington House to Burlington Gardens. © David Chipperfield Architects

91b The Weston Bridge during construction, March 2018. Photo Rory Mulvey

92 Bookshelves in the Library of the Royal Academy, Burlington House. © Royal Academy of Arts, London. Photo Marcus J. Leith

94–95 Key to General Assembly of the Royal Academicians in the entrance hall, Burlington Gardens, 19 March 2018. Photo Johnnie Shand Kydd

All numerals refer to page numbers: those in italic type indicate illustrations

'Abstract Expressionism' (2016) *2–3*
'Africa: Art of a Continent' (1995) 82
Aikman, William, *William Kent 52*
Albert, Prince 49
Angerstein, John Julius 41
Annual Dinner 72, 74
Annual Exhibitions 18, 25, 26, 29, 37, 42, 47, 61
Athens 17; Parthenon 41
Ayling, Stephen *55*

Banks and Barry, architectural firm 54
BBC Home Service 72
Beaumont, Sir George 37, 72
Bicentenary Exhibition (1968) 74
Blake, William 8
Blomfield, Sir Reginald, RA 67
Botticelli, Sandro, *The Birth of Venus* 69
Boyle, Richard, 3rd Earl of Burlington 49, 50
'British Art' (1934) 70
British Museum 54, 87; Museum of Mankind 87; Reading Room 54
Buckingham Palace 67
Burlington Gardens 61, 82, *82*, *90*, *91*
Burlington House *4*, *6*, 13, *48*, 49–58, *51–53*, 64, 74, 77; Annenberg Courtyard *6*, 54; Gallery III *56–57*, 58; great staircase *4*, 50; Jillian and Arthur M. Sackler Wing of Galleries 77, *79–81*; John Madejski Fine Rooms *53*; main galleries 54–58, *56–57*; Saloon *53*
Burlington, 3rd Earl of *see* Boyle, Richard

Campbell, Colen 50, 54, *55*
Caro, Sir Anthony 82
Casson, Sir Hugh, PRA *76*, 77
Cavendish, Lord George 50
Chambers, Sir William, RA 17, 21, 25
Chapman, Jake and Dinos 82
'China: The Three Emperors' (2005) 87
'Chinese Art' (1935) 70
Chipperfield, Sir David, RA 90; Benjamin West Lecture Theatre 91, *91*; link bridge between Burlington House and Burlington Gardens 90, *92*
Chiswick House 50
Churchill, Sir Winston, Hon RA Extraordinary 72
Civil Service Commission 87
Clausen, Sir George, RA 67
Constable, John, RA 8, 29, 37; *A Boat Passing a Lock* 29, *31*; *The Leaping Horse* 29, *32–33*
Cope, Charles West, RA, *The Council of the Royal Academy Selecting Pictures for the Exhibition, 1875* 58–59, *59*
Council of the Royal Academy 8
Courtauld Institute Galleries 25
Craig-Martin, Michael, RA *88–89*

'David Hockney: A Bigger Picture' (2012) *84–85*, 87
Deacon, Richard, RA *80–81*
de Grey, Sir Roger, PRA 77
Denham, Sir John 50
Dicksee, Sir Frank, PRA 67
Diploma Galleries 54, 77
Diploma Works 7, 29, 54
Dowson, Sir Philip, PRA 82
Drury, Alfred, RA 21
'Dutch Art' (1929) 67

Eastlake, Sir Charles Lock, PRA 47, 49, 64
Edward VII, King 64
Elizabeth II, Queen 74
Emin, Tracey, RA 82
Epstein, Jacob 70
'Exhibition of Italian Art' (1930) 67–69, *68*

Festival of Britain (1951) 77
First World War *66*, 67

Flaxman, John, RA 54
Florence 17, 69
Foster of Thames Bank, Lord, RA 77; Foster + Partners *79*
'French Art' (1932) 70
Friends of the Royal Academy 77, 78
Frith, William Powell, RA, *A Private View at the Royal Academy, 1881* 61, *64*

Gainsborough, Thomas, RA 29, 34; *Romantic Landscape with Sheep at a Spring 30*
genre painting 26
Geological Society of London 54
George III, King 7, 17, 21, 37
George IV, King 37
Giampietrino 37; copy of Leonardo's *Last Supper* 37, *38–39*
Gibbs, James 50, *55*
Gibson, John, RA 54
Gilbert & George RA *86*
Giorgione, *La Tempesta* 69
Gladstone, William 61
Grant, Sir Francis, PRA 49, 59, 61; *Self-portrait 51*
Great Exhibition (1851) 49
Great Room, New Somerset House 25, *28*, 58
Grimshaw, Sir Nicholas, PPRA 87; Eurostar terminal, Waterloo Station 87

Handel, George Frideric 50
Hirst, Damien 82
history painting 26
Hockney, David, RA *84–85*, 87
Holland Park 61
Honorary Fellows of the Royal Academy 8
Honorary Royal Academicians 8
Hopkins, Sir Michael, RA 90
Hutchison, Sidney C. 58

Instrument of Foundation 17, *20*

Jackson, Mason, *Taking in the Pictures at the RA 42–43*
Jervis, Simon 8
Jillian and Arthur M. Sackler Wing of Galleries 77, *79–81*
John, Augustus, RA 70
Jones, Inigo 21

Kauffman, Angelica, RA 21, 25, 74
Keeper of the Royal Academy 8, 21
Kelly, Sir Gerald, PRA 72
Kent, William 41, 50, *52*; interiors at Burlington House 50, *53*; King's Mews 41
King, Phillip, PPRA 82
Kip, Johannes *51*
Knight, Dame Laura, RA 74
Knyff, Leonard *51*

landscape painting 26
Langtry, Lillie 61
Laocoön and His Sons (Vatican Museums) 25
Lawrence, Sir Thomas, PRA 37, 38, 41; *Self-portrait 36*
Le Brun, Christopher, PRA *86*, 87
Leigh, Mike 34; *Mr Turner* (2014 film) 34, *34–35*
Leighton, Frederic, Baron Leighton of Stretton, PRA 59, *60*, 61–64; Leighton House, Holland Park Road 61
Leonardo da Vinci 37, 54; *The Last Supper* 37; *The Madonna and Child with St Anne and St John the Baptist*, the Burlington House Cartoon 72–74, *73*, *75*
Lewis, Wyndham 70; *T. S. Eliot 70*
Library of the Royal Academy *9*, 13, *92*
Life Room 8, *10–11*, 21
Linnean Society of London 54
Llewellyn, Sir William, PRA 67, 70
loan exhibitions 8, 58, 67, 78–82
Louis XIV, King 17

Lutyens, Sir Edwin, PRA 70–71, *70*; Cenotaph, Whitehall 71; Viceroy's House, New Delhi 71
Lutyens, Robert, *Sir Edwin Lutyens* *70*

Madejski, John 52
Malton, Thomas *24*
Mantegna, Andrea, *Lamentation over the Dead Christ* 69
Martini, Pietro Antonio *28*
Matisse, Henri 72
Medici, Cosimo de' 17
Medici, Lorenzo de' 17
Michelangelo Buonarroti 37, 54; *The Virgin and Child with the Infant St John*, the Taddei Tondo 37, *39*, 72
Milan 69
Millais, Sir John Everett, Bt PRA 59, 64; *John Ruskin* *46*; *Ophelia* *46*
'Monet in the Twentieth Century' (1999) 82
Monnington, Sir Thomas, PRA 74
Moore, Henry 82
Moser, George Michael, RA 21
Moser, Mary, RA 21, 25, 74
Munnings, Sir Alfred, PRA 71, *71*
Museum of Mankind 87
Mussolini, Benito 67–68

Nash, John 41
National Antarctic Expedition 87
National Art Collections Fund 74
National Gallery 37, *40*, 41, *44–45*, 47, 49, 64, 74
New Delhi 71
New Sculpture 64
'A New Spirit in Painting' (1981) 77, *78*
Newton, Francis Milner, RA 21

Officers of the Royal Academy 8

Pall Mall 18, 21, 29, 41; 125 Pall Mall *16*, 18, 25
Palladio, Andrea 50
Paris 17; Académie Royale de Peinture et de Sculpture 17
Payne, William, *Private View at the Royal Academy* *43*
Pennethorne, Sir James 61, 87
'Persian Exhibition' (1931) 69
Phidias 54
Philip, Prince 74
Picasso, Pablo 72
Piccadilly 49, 50, 59
Plato 17
Pope, Alexander 50
portraiture 26
Poynter, Sir Edward, Bt PRA 64, 67
Pre-Raphaelite Brotherhood 47
President of the Royal Academy 8, 35, 47, 49, 70, 71, 74, 77, 82, 87; medal 37, *86*
Punch 47

Ramberg, Johann Heinrich *28*
Raphael 54
'The Real Van Gogh: The Artist and His Letters' (2010) 87
Renouard, Charles Paul, *The Royal Academy* *62–63*
Reynolds, Sir Joshua, PRA 17, 21, 26, 37, 54; *Discourses* 21, 26; *King George III* *18*; *Self-portrait* *20*; *Sir William Chambers* *19*
Ricci, Sebastiano 50
Richardson, Sir Albert, PRA 72
Rome 17, 37; Compagnia di San Luca (later the Accademia di San Luca) 17
Rosenthal, Sir Norman 77, 78
Rowlandson, Thomas 25; *The Exhibition 'Stare-Case', Somerset House* *27*
Royal Academicians 7, 8, *14–15*, 34, 58–59, 67, 74, 90, *94–95*
Royal Academy Schools 8, 18, 25, 37, 38, 42, 49, 59–61, 64, 67, 72; camouflage for naval ships 67; Professors 8
Royal Astronomical Society 54

Royal Society of Chemistry 54
Ruskin, John *46*, 47

Saatchi, Charles 82
Sackler Wing of Galleries *see* Jillian and Arthur M. Sackler Wing of Galleries
St James's Palace 17
St John's Wood 61
St Martin-in-the-Fields 41
St Paul's Cathedral 37
Santa Maria delle Grazie, Milan 37
Sargent, John Singer, RA, *Henry James* 67
Saumarez Smith, Charles 87
Second World War 71
Secretary of the Royal Academy 21, 58
Secretary and Chief Executive of the Royal Academy 8, 87
Senior Royal Academicians 8
'Sensation: Young British Artists from the Saatchi Collection' (1997) 82, *83*
Shaw, Richard Norman, RA 61
Shee, Sir Martin Archer, PRA 38, 47
Sickert, Walter, RA 70; *Santa Maria della Salute 69*
Singleton, Henry 25; *The Royal Academicians in General Assembly* 25, *26*
Smirke, Sir Robert, RA 54
Smirke, Sydney, RA 54, *56–57*, 58, *59–61*, 67, 77, 87
Society of Antiquaries of London 54
Somerset House, New *24*, 25, 38; Great Room 25, *28*, 58
Somerset House, Old 21, 25
South Kensington 49
'Spanish Art' (1920) 67
Spectator 77
Spencer, Sir Stanley, RA 70
still-life painting 26
Strand *24*, 25, 70
suffragettes 67
Summer Exhibition 7, 58, 59, 61, 67, 70, 71, *88–89*

Taddei family 37
Terry, Ellen 61
Thornycroft, Sir Hamo, RA, *Teucer 65*
Titian 54
Trafalgar Square 18, 38, *40*, 41, 42, 49
Treasurer of the Royal Academy 8, 18, 54
Trollope, Anthony 61
Turner, J. M. W., RA 8, 29, *34–35*, 35, 37, 47; *Dolbadern Castle* 29, *30*

University of London 61, 87

Varnishing Days 29, 34
Veneto 50
Venice 50, 69
Victoria, Queen 49, 61, 64

Watts, George Frederick, RA, *Frederic, Lord Leighton PRA 60*
Webb, Sir Aston, PRA 67
West, Benjamin, PRA 21, 25, 35–37; *Self-portrait 36*
Wheeler, Sir Charles, PRA 72
Wilde, Oscar 61
Wilkins, William, RA 41, *44–45*
William IV, King 41
William of Wykeham, Bishop of Winchester 54
Wilson, Sir Colin St John, RA 90
Winter Exhibitions 58
Wren, Sir Christopher 54
Wyatt, James, PRA 35

Young British Artists 82, *83*

Zoffany, Johann, RA 21; *The Academicians of the Royal Academy* 21, *22–23*

British Library Cataloguing-in-Publication Data
A catalogue record for this book is available from the British Library

ISBN 978-1-910350-97-3

Distributed outside the United States and Canada by ACC Art Books Ltd, Riverside House, Dock Lane, Melton, Woodbridge, Suffolk IP12 1PE

Distributed in the United States and Canada by ACC Art Books, 6 West 18th Street, Suite 4B, New York, NY 10011

For R.A.J.S. (1940–2018)

Acknowledgements
I am exceptionally grateful to Mark Pomeroy, Nick Savage, Helen Valentine and Annette Wickham for their wise improvements to the text, and to Rebecca Penmore and my five publishing colleagues for their invaluable work on the book's design and production.

Royal Academy Publications
Florence Dassonville
Alison Hissey
Rosie Hore
Carola Krueger
Peter Sawbridge
Nick Tite

Design: Rebecca Penmore
Colour origination: Gomer Press
Printed in Wales by Gomer Press